History of
Emmanuel United Methodist Church

Compiled By
Bill McLaughlin

Waldenhouse Publishers, Inc.
Walden, Tennessee

History of Emmanuel United Methodist Church

Copyright © 2021 Bill McLaughlin. All rights reserved. No part of this book may be reproduced in any form or by any electronic or mechanical means including information storage and retrieval systems, without permission in writing from the publisher. The only exception is by a reviewer, who may quote short excerpts in a review.

Compiled by: Bill McLaughlin

Cover design by: Leslie Bouldin

Published by Waldenhouse Publishers, Inc.

100 Clegg Street, Signal Mountain, Tennessee 37377 USA

423-886-2721 www.waldenhouse.com

Type and Design by Karen Paul Stone

Printed in the United States of America

ISBN: 978-1-947589-65-0

Library of Congress Control Number: 2022947190

  History of Emmanuel United Methodist Church in East Memphis, Tennessee, is a
  display of vision, faith, and commitment of all those who attended and served from
  its beginning in 1968 through the first fifty years. Contains 82 historic documents,
  photographs and drawings. -- provided by Publisher

HIS036120 HISTORY / United States / State & Local / South

HIS036000 HISTORY / United States / General

REL016000 RELIGION / Institutions & Organizations

Introduction

The information presented herein is a picture of faith and courage. The growth of the Church and its outreach must have surpassed the vision and imagination of those early members who gathered to rise-up and build. Certainly, God has been with this Church as it has extended its mission throughout the community, city, and world.

In order to understand the history and development of Emmanuel, we must take our minds back, 50+ years ago to that period of time in East Memphis. The property we see today was primarily woods with subdivision development just beginning with some houses under construction. Families were beginning to look and move eastward.

Thoughts of a new church in East Memphis began to develop in late 1967. Early in the spring of 1968, Dr. F. A. Flat, District Superintendent of the Memphis Shelby District, as it was known at the time, began to formulate plans to establish a new church unit of the Methodist Church on a sight purchased by the Metro Missionary Society, which was part of the district.

Contents

Illustrations

Early Methodism in West Tennessee
The Wesley Circuit Trail in Shelby and Tipton Counties

Wesley is an old Crossroad town two miles west of present-day Stanton. It was at the crossroads of the Memphis-Brownsville Road and the Somerville-Randolph Road. There is a state historical marker on Highway 70 near Wesley. This was not only a wayside service place for stage and cotton wagons but also an early Methodist evangelization place. There was an early church here and by 1840 it was made a large circuit with pastors residing here when not traveling. They served churches in Haywood, Fayette, Tipton, and Shelby Counties.

Wesley diminished in importance as the port town of Randolph became less important and the Louisville and Nashville Railroad finished linking to Bartlett and Memphis. An acre or more in an old Wesley Cemetery mark the crossroads today with large trees in it. But during the years 1840 to 1870, it was one of the largest circuits in West Tennessee Methodist history. Because of some faithful Methodist in Stanton, TN some of the old official records of its quarterly conference still exist.

Wesley Circuit served churches south of the Hatchie River bottoms and North and East of Wolf River. These rivers were troublesome to navigate, especially in the winter. From Wesley there were "high ground" roads or trails to Raleigh, Munford (Mt. Zion), Poplar Grove Bethel, Embury, Macedonia, Gratitude, Pleasant Ridge (1824), Clopton, Pleasant Grove at Gainesville, Old Sharon, Old Concordia near Braden, and Warren's Chapel (or old Pisgah) near Bartlett.

An earlier circuit was called Wolf River Circuit operating out of Memphis or Raleigh from 1825 to 1839. Serving people north of Wolf River and Loosahatchie River must have been very difficult in wet weather, although there was an early crossing at Raleigh and on Second Street near the Mississippi River on a road toward Covington.

The northern part of the county was only served by the Wolf River Circuit from 1825 to 1839. Then with the formation of the Memphis Conference in 1840, the Wesley Circuit was formed to better reach these areas. In turn, the Memphis District and Circuits reached all areas south of Wolf River, reaching deep into Mississippi, which was now a part of the Memphis Conference, from 1840 to 1870.

From Wesley Circuit, there were preaching places in all directions south of the Big Hatchie River. Early appointments were at Covington, Hebron, Tabernacle and Charleston in Tipton County. Then moving toward Memphis, there were Methodists at Galloway, Old Sharon (1833), north of Mason Station, where there was a good congregation of Blacks as well as Whites. Pleasant Grove at Gainesville also became a church for Blacks early on. The Alexander Chapel Church had its own building as early as 1847 when Sharon built a new building, and the Blacks had full use of their old building north of Mason Station. This may be one of the earliest Black congregations (mostly slaves) who were permitted to meet independently (1847). Their name came later as a school was founded for the freed Blacks after the Civil War and their teacher/preacher was Charles Alexander, a Methodist Episcopal minister from the North, who worked among them with school and church.

Concordia Church north and west of Braden was another stop for the preachers and this was quite a nice congregation for many years. It is considered the mother church for Braden as Sharon is for Mason. Not far away in Fayette County, the Bellemont Church was a main stop and a strong church and leader of a circuit for many years. Reaching Shelby County, there were Methodist families at Gratitude and a church and school there in the early 1840's and at Macedonia also.

Further toward Memphis, there was the village at Brunswick with known Methodist connections, and the Warren, Chapel (or Old Pisgah) dating back to 1837 or earlier with a welcome to traveling preachers. The better road to Memphis led through

Raleigh which had been a favorite hunting and camping place for Chickasaw Indians prior to the entrance of White men as early as 1812. The older part of Davies Plantation Log House is reputed to be the hunting lodge of an Indian Chief.

Raleigh was an early place to get help crossing Wolf River on the way to Memphis and was a healthier climate than Memphis along the river. It was a natural place for business, pleasure and preaching. Their records tell of visiting preachers early on and by 1836 they had built a Methodist house of worship which was used by other churches also. Raleigh was also the seat of county government for some years. Even after Memphis became the county seat, the State Circuit Court preferred to meet in Raleigh and after Bartlett became the nearest railway station (1857), the Circuit Court met in Bartlett several years.

Some five miles south of Bartlett, Charles Bryan Road at Raleigh-LaGrange Road, there was a Methodist congregation and building believed to have begun in 1840 and continued until the building burned in 1914. It must have been served and perhaps started by the Wesley Circuit Riders. This was also plantation land and there would have been Blacks as well as Whites to evangelize. An old cemetery there marks the spot, and another denomination has a church there now.

Two rural churches have searched out their histories through early settlers that came to West Tennessee with slaves to develop cotton plantations. They are Clopton United Methodist Church (1831) in southern Tipton County and Pleasant Ridge (1825) in Shelby County. Clopton records indicate that their ministers were on the Wesley Circuit from 1840 to 1869. The Clopton Church lists their pastors from 1836-1839 from the Wolf River Circuit. The Pleasant Ridge church started about 1825 by the Methodist families of Thomas and John B. Person, brothers who bought 10,000 acres of land in Shelby County and moved their families and slaves to Pleasant Ridge in 1820-1821. Earlier services were held in their homes but by 1825 they built a log cabin near the John B. Person home especially for preaching services and Sunday School.

Bethuel at Kerrville dates back to the 1840's and has a large Bethuel cemetery. Munford and Campground churches date from the 1840's also and were on the Wesley Circuit. Poplar Grove in extreme southwest Tipton County was also an appointment for the Wesley Circuit. Bethuel later became a leader for a circuit as did Raleigh and Clopton, Munford (Mt. Zion) became the leader for a circuit for Tipton County and later a District High School was established there which later became a public school for Tipton County.

Concordia and Bellemont became leaders for circuits in later years also. Galloway and Mason became center for the Methodist Episcopal North Mission Churches among the Blacks after 1866. Alexander Chapel is most likely the oldest Black congregation in West Tennessee Methodist history. The Methodist Episcopal Church came after the Civil War and records have not been well documented but there were churches at Galloway, Mason, Pleasant Grove, Atoka Lucy (Friendship), Centenary, Burdette and others.

> "I AM NOT AFRAID THAT THE PEOPLE CALLED METHODIST SHOULD EVER CEASE TO EXIST IN EUROPE OR AMERICA, BUT AM AFRAID LEST THEY SHOULD ONLY EXIST AS A SECT, HAVING THE FORM OF RELIGION WITHOUT POWER. AND THIS UNDOUBTEDLY WILL BE THE CASE UNLESS THEY HOLD FAST BOTH THE DOCTRINE AND SPIRIT"
>
> John Wesley

Statement of John Wesley

EUMC
Mission Statement

You shall love the Lord your God with all your heart, and with all your soul, and with all your strength, and with all your mind; and your neighbor as yourself.

EUMC
Vision Statement

Emmanuel United Methodist Church's vision is to be a growing and vital community where Christ is transforming lives.

Emmanuel United Methodist Church

History of Emmanuel United Methodist Church

Compiled
By
Bill McLaughlin
Chairperson – History and Archives
June 2, 2021

The information presented herein is a picture of faith and courage. The growth of the Church and its outreach must have surpassed the vision and imagination of those early members who gathered to rise-up and build. Certainly, God has been with this Church as it has extended its mission throughout the community, city, and world.

In order to understand the history and development of Emmanuel, we must take our minds back, 50+ years ago to that period of time in East Memphis. The property we see today was primarily woods with subdivision development just beginning with some houses under construction. Families were beginning to look and move eastward.

Thoughts of a new church in East Memphis began to develop in late 1967. Early in the spring of 1968, Dr. F. A. Flat, District Superintendent of the Memphis Shelby District, as it was known at the time, began to formulate plans to establish a new church unit of the Methodist Church on a sight purchased by the Metro Missionary Society, which was part of the district.

A plat and Quit Claim Deed, shown on the following pages, convey the land on which the church was to be built, to the trustees of Emmanuel United Methodist Church.

EXHIBIT A

This Instrument Prepared By:
Harold C. Curry, Attorney
12 South Main Street
Memphis, Tennessee

QUIT CLAIM DEED   EG 4851

THIS INDENTURE, made and entered into this 15 day of December, 1969
by and between CLIFFORD D. PIERCE, DOYLE C. HANCE and J. ELLINGTON THOMAS,
Trustees of the MEMPHIS DISTRICT OF THE MEMPHIS CONFERENCE OF THE UNITED METH-
ODIST CHURCH and HAROLD C. CURRY, JAMES H. SPARROCK and C. A. DAVIS, Trustees
of the MEMPHIS SHELBY DISTRICT OF THE MEMPHIS CONFERENCE OF THE UNITED METHODIST
CHURCH, allacting as Trustees of and for the use and benefit of YOUNG METROPOLI-
TAN MISSIONARY SOCIETY OF THE UNITED METHODIST CHURCH, parties of the first part
and C. R. WATSON, JR., BENJAMIN R. WALLER, JR., JOHN HUNTER and S. K. McKENZIE,
Trustees of and for EMMANUEL UNITED METHODIST CHURCH, parties of the second part,

WITNESSETH:

THAT WHEREAS, the parties of the first part herein acquired the property
hereinafter described for the purpose of establishing a new Methodist Church
which will eventually occupy the property; and

WHEREAS, Emmanuel United Methodist Church has now been organized and
it is proper for said property to be turned over to the Trustees of said newly
organized church;

NOW THEREFORE, in consideration of the sum of ONE DOLLAR ($1.00) cash in
hand paid, receipt whereof is hereby acknowledged, and of the premises recited
herein, and of the desire of the parties of the first part to vest title to said
property in the parties of the second part, the parties of the first part do hereby remise, release, quit claim and convey unto the said parties of the second
part all of their right, title, claim and interest of every kind and character
in and to the following described real estate situated and being in the SECOND
CIVIL DISTRICT of Shelby County, Tennessee, to-wit:

Lots 1, 2 and 3 of Clarkwood Subdivision, as shown on plat recorded in Plat
Book 21, page 17 in the Register's Office of Shelby County, Tennessee, to which
recorded plat reference is made for a more particular description.

Being the same property described in and conveyed by warranty deed recorded in
Book 6280, page 584 in said Register's Office.

The name of The Methodist Church has now been officially changed to The United
Methodist Church.

TO HAVE AND TO HOLD the aforesaid real estate, together with all the appur-
tenances and hereditaments thereunto belonging or any wise appertaining unto the
said parties of the second part, their successors and assigns in fee simple for-
ever, in trust that said premises shall be used, kept and maintained as a place
of divine worship of the United Methodist Ministry and Members of The United
Methodist Church; subject to the discipline, usage, and ministerial appointments
of said church as from time to time authorized and declared by the general conference and by the annual conference within whose bounds the said premises are
situated. This provision is solely for the benefit of the Grantee herein and
the Grantor reserves no right or interest in said premises.

IN WITNESS WHEREOF the parties of the first part have signed their names
on this the day and year first above written.

_____   _____
TRUSTEE   TRUSTEE

_____   _____
TRUSTEE   TRUSTEE

_____   _____
TRUSTEE   TRUSTEE

TRUSTEES OF THE MEMPHIS DISTRICT OF THE   TRUSTEES OF THE MEMPHIS SHELBY DISTRICT
MEMPHIS CONFERENCE OF THE UNITED METHO-   OF THE MEMPHIS CONFERENCE OF THE UNITED
DIST CHURCH   METHODIST CHURCH

STATE OF TENNESSEE)   E6 4851
COUNTY OF SHELBY)

    Before me, the undersigned Notary Public in and for said State and County
duly commissioned and qualified, personally appeared CLIFFORD D. PIERCE, DOYLE
C. RANCE and J. ELLINGTON THOMAS, Trustees of the MEMPHIS DISTRICT OF THE MEMPHIS
CONFERENCE OF THE UNITED METHODIST CHURCH and HAROLD C. CURRY, JAMES R. SEABROOK,
and C. A. DAVIS, Trustees of the MEMPHIS SHELBY DISTRICT OF THE MEMPHIS CONFER-
ENCE OF THE UNITED METHODIST CHURCH, all acting as Trustees of and for the use
and benefit of MEMPHIS METROPOLITAN MISSIONARY SOCIETY OF THE UNITED METHODIST
CHURCH, to me known to be the persons described in and who executed the foregoing
instrument and acknowledged what they executed the same as their free act and
deed.

    WITNESS my hand and Notarial Seal at office this ___ day of _____,
1969.

My commission expires:
___ March 1970

                                              _____
                                              Notary Public

I, or we hereby swear or affirm that
to the best of affiant's knowledge,
information, and belief, the actual
consideration for this transfer is
less than $50.00.

                            _____
                            Affiant

    Sworn to and subscribed before
me this ___ day of _____,
19__.
                      _____
         Notary Public, Shelby County,
MY COMMISSION EXPIRES SEPT. 28, 1970   Tennessee
    State Tax $ 0.00
    Clerk's fee   0.00
    Recording fee 5.00
    Total $ 5.00

    TO#148831, H. Curry

Parcels 81-26-17
         81-26-18
         81-26-16

STATE TAX
RECORDED
REC.
Dec 31 3 21 PM
STATE OF TENNESSEE

E6 4851

On the following pages are pictures of each of the ministers who served Emmanuel United Methodist Church together with the dates of their tenure.

Each minister brought with them their own style, their own commitment, their own love for Emmanuel. Each one was unique with different personalities, different strengths and weaknesses, and each one appeared to possess their own objective. These characteristics, are to some degree, reflected in the progress the church was able to achieve during their ministry at Emmanuel.

The bishop and his/her cabinet, along with some guidance and direction from the local church pastoral committee, decide upon and make pastoral appointments to each church annually. The appointments, while made annually, generally extend the tenure to multiple years.

Emmanuel has had eight ministers in its fifty-year history, an average tenure of six years. The longest term was thirteen years and the shortest was three and one-half years. The individual ministers also provided some input which may or may not agree with the bishop and the cabinet's decision. This must be an awesome task given the number of churches and pastoral families that must be considered each year.

Most often the appointments work well between the church and pastoral families. However, there are and have been times at Emmanuel, as well as other churches, when the appointments did not appear proper for the church at the appointed time.

Of interest is the fact that in earlier years, the appointments of ministers were made at annual conference. The ministers did not know for sure if they would be moving to a new venue or remaining with their current church. If they were to be moving, they would be expected to be out of the parsonage and have it cleaned for the new pastoral family by the middle of the following week. This would provide only three or four days for the pastor and family to pack, move and clean. Obviously, this put pressure on ministers to organize and coordinate their move as it would usually involve several families. Today, appointments are made earlier and most ministers know, prior to annual conference, if they will be moving and where.

Two pastors of Emmanuel were moved to the district superintendent position, one during mid-year. Changes like this, while necessary, affect the progress of programs within the church. There were two ministers who retired after serving their appointments to Emmanuel.

While it is the belief of some that the true and factual events that occurred through the years in Emmanuel's history should be included herein, others feel that only the positive events should be included.

In an effort not to be unfair or judgmental or include something that would cause consternation for any minister or Emmanuel, only a brief amount of narrative has been written as regards to each minister.

Accordingly, nothing has been included within this history to discuss the growth or decline in membership, giving and attendance during the tenure of individual ministers. Graphs and charts have been included to assist the reader in tracking these areas through the years if one so desires.

Reverend Ken Burnette 1968-81

Reverend Harold Watkins 1981-1986

Dr. Dave Hilliard 1986-1995

Reverend Tommy Edwards 1995-2001

Reverend Barry Henson 2001-2007

Reverend Larry Daniel 2007 - 2010

Dr. David Comperry 2010-2017

Dr. Wade Cox 2017 - present

Organization in 1968

A meeting was held at Underwood Methodist Church on Good Friday, April 12, 1968 at 7:30 PM for the purpose of discussing a steering committee and formulation of the new church.

A second meeting was held in the Memphis University School Chapel on May 5, 1968 at 2:30 PM to appoint a steering committee for the new Methodist Church. The following were selected to serve: Mr. and Mrs. Armie Haines, Mr. and Mrs. John Hunter, Mr. Bill Lewis, Mr. and Mrs. Tom Marshall, Mr. Ben Waller Jr., Mr. and Mrs. Charles Watson and Mr. and Mrs. Walker Wilkerson. Mr. Ben Waller, Jr. was elected to serve as chairman. Others attending included Dr. Flatt, DS, Mr. Bill Smith of the district office, and Rev. Ken Burnette.

The evening of May 11, 1968, Bishop Ellis Finger, Jr., Resident Bishop of the Nashville area, invited to a dinner at Memphis University School, all who were interested in the new church. At that dinner, plans were made for the first worship service to be held Sunday morning, June 2nd, 1968. Bishop Finger also announced that Rev. Ken C. Burnette would be appointed to serve as minister.

Reverend Ken Burnette was appointed by the conference to be Emmanuel's founding minister. Reverend Burnette, his wife Virginia and four daughters, Sara, Ann, Nancy, and Rebecca moved into a small house on the church property and lived there until August 9, 1968, when a parsonage was purchased for $36,500. Reverend Burnette started his tenure at Emmanuel after serving Munford United Methodist Church. Being a new church, Emmanuel had a limited staff and was burdened financially. Reverend Burnette was gifted at multiple tasks and he, along with members, were often required to perform many of the chores in and around the church.

On June 2, 1968, Emmanuel Methodist Church was officially organized. On that first Sunday, 67 people were received into the membership. In the evening of June 2, 1968, the church held its first official meeting. The members who had joined in the morning service were nominated and approval was given for the positions to be filled as shown on the pages which follow.

A resolution was passed on June 16, 1968, by the Quarterly Conference of Emmanuel United Methodist Church, which authorized and empowered the trustees to purchase a parsonage located at 6468 Messick Road. A copy of the resolution is included below.

<u>A RESOLUTION</u>

Whereas Emmanuel United Methodist Church does not at this time own a parsonage for the minister and his family,

And whereas it is the accepted policy of the United Methodist Church to so provide housing for its ministers and families,

Be it therefore resolved that the Quarterly Conference of the Emmanuel United Methodist Church in called session on this 16th day of June 1968, after having given due and proper notice of the required ten days, notice being first given to the Church on June 2, 1968, be it resolved that the Quarterly Conference of the Emmanuel United Methodist Church empower and direct its Trustees to purchase an adequate parsonage.

Be it futher resolved that the Trustees be empowered to purchase as the parsonage the house located at 6468 Messick Road, lot number 16, in the Keswick Sub-division, Shelby County, Tennessee, such house having been duly examined and unanimously approved by the District Board of Church Locations and Buildings.

Be it further resolved that the Trustees be authorized and empowered to secure a loan with which to pay for the parsonage and give a mortage on the parsonage as security for the loan.

Approved this 16th day of June, 1968.

District Superintendent, Chairman
Of Quarterly Conference.

Secretary of Quarterly Conference

Pastor

First Bulletin — June 2, 1968
Emmanuel United Methodist Church

Renewal at Pentecost

AT THE LOWER LEFT of the mosaic on the cover, the artist has purposely left a portion unfinished, suggesting that God's dream for his world is still unfinished. Jesus said, "My Father is working still, and I am working." "He who believes in me will also do the works that I do."

"As the Father has sent me, even so send I you." Jesus obviously believed God needed men to help him finish his creation. He told his disciples they would have help and guidance as they worked for God's kingdom—that the Holy Spirit would come to them.

On Pentecost, the fiftieth day after the resurrection and the seventh Sunday after Easter, the power of God in the Holy Spirit descended upon them in mighty force—and the world has not been the same since. Those discouraged followers of Jesus soon to be called Christians were so changed and empowered that everywhere they went they turned the world upside down, or rather right side up.

On this Pentecost Sunday, if we are filled with the Spirit, live in the Spirit, and walk in the Spirit, we can be empowered to do our part in working with God on his unfinished world, helping him create that "new earth" wherein dwelleth righteousness, brotherhood, and peace.

On the Cover: "Foreseeing the World," a mosaic by Prather, Christ Church, Washington, D.C.

The kingdom of the world has become the kingdom of our Lord and of his Christ, and he shall reign for ever and ever. —Revelation 11:15 RSV

EMMANUEL UNITED METHODIST CHURCH
Meeting In Hyde Memorial Chapel
Memphis University School

Ken Burnette   Minister

Morning Worship   10:30 A.M.   June 2, 1968

"Ye shall seek me, and find me, when ye shall search
for me with all your heart."
    - Jeremiah 29:13

The Prelude   Mrs. Charles Shutte
Call To Worship   Dr. F. A. Flatt
*Hymn "The Church's One Foundation" (1,2,4) No. 381
*Affirmation Of Faith (The Apostle's Creed)   In Unison
Music For Meditation   The Pianist
*The Responsive Reading (First Reading) Page 592
    "The Mind Of Christ"

*Gloria Patri   In Unison
The Scripture Lesson   Acts 2: 37-47
The Pastoral Prayer   The Lord's Prayer
Announcements
Worship In Tithes And Offerings
   Offertory Prayer   The Minister
   Offertory   The Pianist
*Doxology   In Unison
Special Music   Dr. Cecil L. Raines
The Sermon   Rev. Ken Burnette
    "A CHURCH ON THE MOVE"

Invitation To Christian Discipleship
*Hymn "I Love Thy Kingdom, Lord" (1,2,3)   No. 379
The Reception of Members   The Ministers
The Benediction   Dr. F. A. Flatt

THE ACT OF OFFICIALLY ORGANIZING THE CHURCH
The Constituting Church Conference   Dr. F. A. Flatt
The First Quarterly Conference   Dr. F. A. Flatt
    ****

* (The Congregation will please stand).

We Express Our Gratitude to Dr. F. A. Flatt, District
Superintendent, to Mr. Bill Smith, chairman of the
Church Extension Committee of the Memphis Metropolitan
Missionary Society, and to a very faithful steering
committee whose untiring efforts have led to this day.

Emmanuel United Methodist Church is being sponsored
by the Methodist churches in Memphis and Shelby County
through the Memphis Metropolitan Missionary Society.
The Society has:
- Purchased the six acre lot at Kirby & Mossick roads.
- Agreed to pay the Minister's salary for one year.
- Agreed to give $11,000 as down payment on a parson-
  age and $3,000 for furnishings for the parsonage.
- Paid $1,800 rent for Hyde Memorial Chapel, M. U. S.
  for one year.
- Agreed to give a minimum of $50,000 toward the con-
  struction of the first unit.

Reception Of Members: At the conclusion of the sermon, an invitation to join this church will be extended
to all present. All who want to unite with this church
in this very first service will be asked to come forward. So that accurate records may be kept, you are
asked to fill in the enclosed card and bring it as you
come. Members will be received in any way in which we,
as Methodists, receive members: by profession of Faith
and baptism, by transfer of membership from another
Methodist Church or from any other denomination, or by
renewal of vows to Christ and His Church.

We Welcome each of you to this historic occasion.
May the worship and other experiences of this day be
enriching in your life. You are invited to worship
each Sunday and become an active part of this church.

We Express our sincere thanks to Mrs. Charles Shutte,
our pianist, and to Dr. Cecil Raines, our soloist. We
are grateful for the service they have rendered in making our worship service more meaningful.

Visitation: Monday and Thursday evenings, teams
will be visiting prospects in the community. Everyone
who will participate is invited to meet at the home of
Mr. Bill Lewis at 7:00 p.m.

The Ushers For Today: A. B. Haines, John Helder,
Bill Lewis, and Walker Wilkerson.

The Welcoming Committee in the vestibule includes:
Mr. & Mrs. John Hunter and Mr. & Mrs. Ted McKenzie.

First Report of The Nominating Committee
June 2, 1968

For Elective Stewards

Mr. A. B. Haines	Mr. Ted McKenzie	Mr. J. Lee Vestal
Mrs. A. B. Haines	Mrs. Ted McKenzie	Mrs. Lee Vestal
Mr. W. L. Lewis	Mr. Tom Marshall	Mr. Ben Waller
Mr. John Heider	Mr. John Hunter	Mr. Charles Watson
Mrs. John Heider	Mr. John Van Deren	Mrs. Charles Watson
Mr. W.B. Wilkerson	Dr. James Goldschmidt	

For Trustees

Mr. John Hunter	Mr. Charles Watson
Mr. Ted McKenzie	Mr. Ben Waller

For Church School Superintendent
Mr. W. B. Wilkerson

For Children's Superintendent
Mrs. Charles Watson

For Youth Superintendent
Mr. Lee Vestal

For Charge Lay Leader
Mr. W. L. Lewis

For Chairman of Commission on Stewardship and Finance
Mr. Charles Watson

For Chairman of Commission on Membership and Evangelism
Mr. W. L. Lewis

For Church Treasurer
Mr. John Hunter

Respectfully Submitted:
Ken Burnette, Pastor, Chairman

A.B. Haines	John Heider
John Hunter	W. L. Lewis

The new church was sponsored by the United Methodist Churches of the Memphis Shelby District. In addition, substantial assistance was provided by the Memphis Annual Conference and the National Board of Missions of the Methodist Church.

It was originally suggested that the name of the new church would be St. Peters, however as we know, Emmanuel (God With Us) was the final choice.

With deep faith, commitment, and determination, this small congregation with limited resources began a journey that would surpass all expectations. Some of the members in attendance that first service continue their Christian service and worship at Emmanuel today. I would mention the Bodie, Goldschmidt, Haines and Springfield families.

The Official Board of Emmanuel Methodist Church met at the Fellowship House on the church property at 7:30 PM on June 24, 1968.

The following officers were elected:

Chairman – Ben Waller, Jr.
Co-Chairman – Jim Goldschmidt
Secretary - Corrine Watson

The following members were elected to serve on the Finance Committee:

Chuck Watson, Chairman
Jim Braden
John Conrad
Armie Haines
Tom Marshall
Ted McKenzie
Lee Vestal

Ex officio members:
John Hunter, Treasurer
Bill Lewis Lay Leader

Attention should be given to the fact that multiple positions were held by these early members.

The early members worshipped in Hyde Chapel of MUS. By May 1969, the membership had grown to 170.

A resolution was adopted at a Church Conference on January 12, 1969 to authorize trustees to borrow $163,341 for the construction of the first building. It was at that point that the congregation gathered under the majestic oaks to break ground for the new church building which was completed in March 1970 and consecrated on June 28, 1970.

The following members were elected to serve on the Building Committee:

Jim Braden	Ted McKenzie
John Conrad	John Van Deren
Armie Haines	Ben Waller
John Heider	Chuck Watson
Bill Lewis	Barbara Wilkerson

With the financial support received, the new membership was able to build a very functional first unit of the master plan. The new building, which included a sanctuary, perimeter classrooms, kitchen at the rear of the sanctuary, and bathrooms, provided sufficient space for worship, study, fellowship, and service projects for a rapidly growing congregation. Rather than pews, folding chairs were set in the sanctuary and could be moved when tables were needed for a special event.

A review of the minutes of the first meetings are quite interesting. Of significance is the fact that during the first year of the church's existence, even before a building was constructed, a clothes closet for the needy was established. This outreach established in the early life of the church continues today.

Ben Waller, Jr's report to the Official Board at the end of the first year included this statement. *"If there were one wish I might have for our church in the coming years it would be this: Considering that it is now well for us to emphasize our growth in membership and the building of our first unit, let us not fail to look outside the walls of our warm fellowship and see that there are needs to be met beyond this fellowship--needs of people in a world to which Christ calls us and will continue to call us in days to come."*

As shown on the following page, it was originally a part of the master plan for the future sanctuary to be constructed on the west side of the first unit. As time passed and needs changed, other plans were made.

For four years, the Metro Missionary Society assisted in supporting Emmanuel financially and spiritually. This group, along with the conference and General Church, invested a total of $164,000 so that Emmanuel could become a self-supporting church.

The support included:

- The purchase of the 5.24 acre church site.
- The initial payment of $11,000 on the parsonage and $3,000 for parsonage furnishings.
- Paying the pastor's salary for one year.
- Paying rent on the use of Hyde Chapel.
- Paying $50,000 toward construction of the first building.

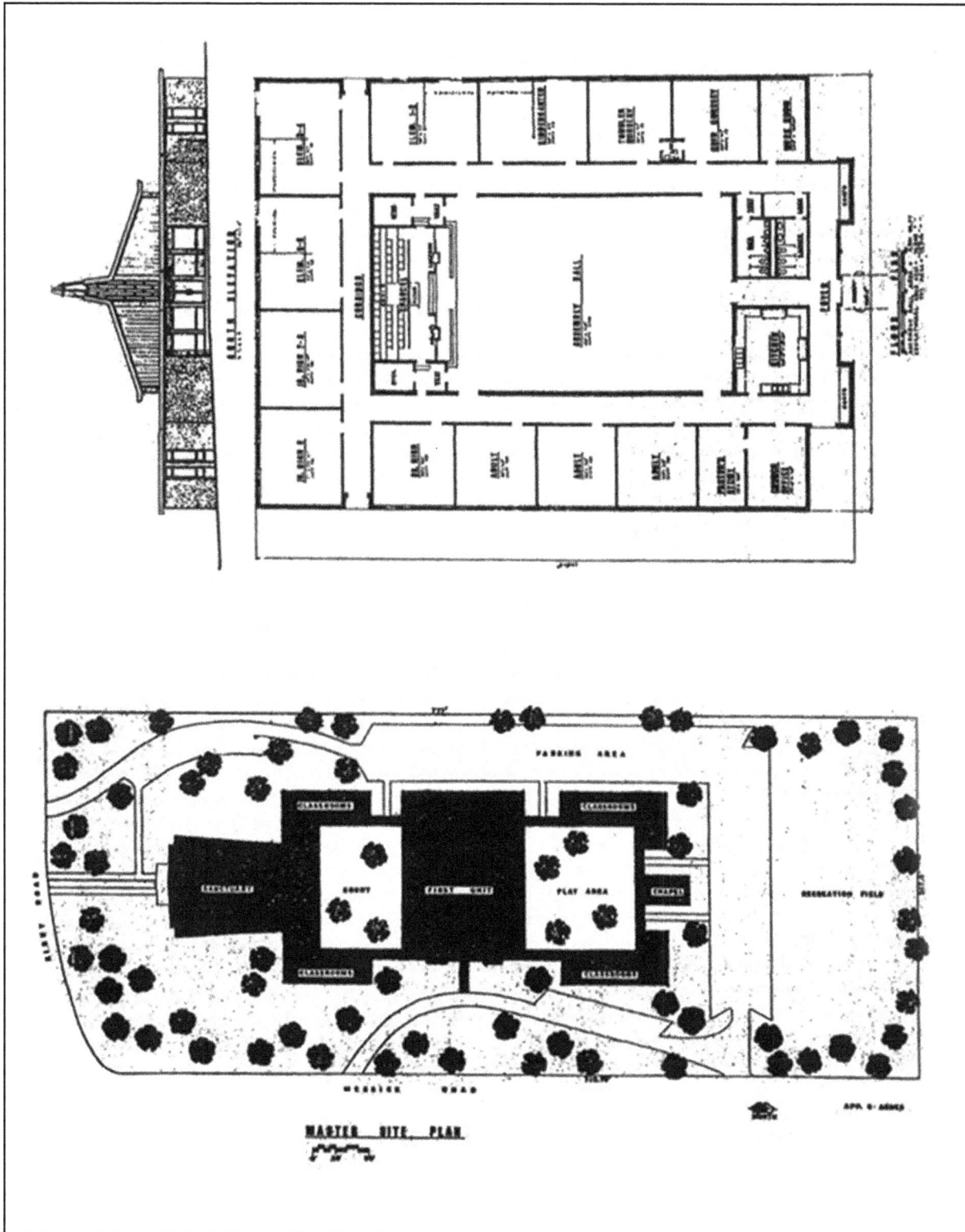

Original Church Floor Plan and Future Planned Sanctuary

Emmanuel United Methodist Church Charter Members

EMMANUEL UNITED METHODIST CHURCH
CHARTER MEMBERS

Bill	Adcock	Susan	Ferguson	Steve	Nash
Joann	Adcock	Wilma	Ferguson	Glenn	Niere
Linda	Adcock	Ethel	Folger	Marilyn	Niere
Howard	Anderson	Wiley	Folger	Robert	Niere
Sue	Anderson	Betty	Goldschmid	Edwin	Pearson
Tim	Anderson	James	Goldschmid	Hilda	Pearson
Barbara	Barker	Anne	Grissom	Jan	Powers
Emmett	Barker	Robert D.	Grissom	Janine	Powers
K. D.	Benjamin	Jo	Haines	William	Powers
Louise	Benjamin	A. B.	Haines, Jr.	Dale	Proctor
Pamela Gail	Benjamin	Janis	Hammermann	Joe F.	Proctor
Harry	Blackford	Marian	Hammermann	Joe	Proctor, III
Jean	Blackford	Frank	Hardison	Don	Quasdorf
Jeffery	Blackford	Gwen	Hardison	Jeanne	Quasdorf
Mark	Blackford	John	Heider	Robert	Quasdorf
Jane	Bodie	John	Heider	Susan	Quasdorf
Jennifer	Bodie	Judy	Heider	Anne	Radcliffe
Suzanne	Bodie	Sandra	Heider	Wanda	Radcliffe
William	Bodie	Carol	Hunter	Drew	Robbins
Bill	Bodie, Jr.	Jean	Hunter	L. O.	Robbins
Audrey	Braden	John	Hunter	Pat	Robbins
James	Braden	John	Hunter, Jr.	Wendy	Robbins
Ben	Briskey	Betty	Kelly	Barbara	Schuette
Dodie	Briskey	James E.	Kelly	Carol	Schuette
Donna	Brown	Diane	Lewis	Charles	Schuette
James	Brown	Eleanor	Lewis	Charles	Schuette, Jr.
Sarah	Burnette	George W.	Lewis	James	Springfield
Virginia	Burnette	Randy	Lewis	Shirley	Springfield
George	Burton	Steve	Lewis	Betty Jo	Thornton
Katherine	Burton	W. L.	Lewis, Jr.	Raymond	Thornton
James B.	Cheatam	Anne	Long	Mary Anne	Tipton
Marilyn	Cheatam	George N.	Long	Ralph	Tipton
Arlyne	Clauson	Donna	Marshall	Adele	VanDeren
Darrell	Clauson	Thomas	Marshall	John	VanDeren, Jr.
Ricky Lee	Clauson	Martha	Massey	Evelyn	Vestal
Sheri	Clauson	Sarah	Massey	Janice	Vestal
Stephen	Clauson	William S.	Massey	Jay L.	Vestal, Jr.
Ann	Conrad	Bill	Massey Jr.	J. Lee	Vestal, Sr.
John	Conrad	Frances	McDaniel	Ginny	Waller
John Lee	Conrad	Robert	McDaniel	Nelle	Waller
Debbie	Davis	Dan	McKenzie	Ben R.	Waller, Jr.
Joy	Davis	Fayne	McKenzie	Corrine	Watson
Walter E.	Davis	Hunter	McKenzie	Charles	Watson, Jr.
Bill	Drumwright	Rebecca	McKenzie	J. H.	Wells
Darla	Drumwright	S. K.	McKenzie	Patricia	Wells
Mary	Drumwright	Wanda	McKenzie	Bobby	White
Cheryle Sue	Duncan	Weesie	McKenzie	Pam	White
Curtis	Duncan	Cheryl Ann	Moore	Patricia	White
Lloyd K.	Duncan	Joanna Gail	Moore	Robert	White
Pat	Duncan	John C.	Moore	Barbara	Wilkerson
Stanley	Duncan	Lou	Moore	Lynn	Wilkerson
Betty	Ellis	Della	Moss	Walter	Wilkerson
Cindy	Ellis	Phillip	Moss	Mrs. Clarence	Williams
Rob	Ellis	Scott	Moss	Hoyt	Wilson
Robert	Ellis	Dudley	Nash	Marilyn	Wilson
Judy	Ferguson	Lucy	Nash		
Sherrill	Ferguson	Stacye	Nash		

Charter Members

Kindergarten

A very vital part of Emmanuel's growth and development should be attributed to its kindergarten. Nelie Waller, the school's founder in 1970, was the wife of Ben Waller, Jr. who was the architect on the first three phases of the church. The first year, the school had only two teachers, Marvel Hutchison and Adele Van Deren, and was open to only 4 and 5 year old children with an enrollment of 30 students. The tuition was $20.00 a month.

By 2001-2002, the school had an enrollment of over three hundred students at all age levels with a tuition of $293.00 per month depending on grade levels. The school has always been under approval of The Human Services Department. In 1987, it was given national accreditation, and in 1993 the school was approved by the Department of Education for the State of Tennessee.

Nelie continued to direct the kindergarten for more than 30 years until her retirement. Emmanuel's kindergarten has always been recognized as one of the best in Memphis. It is a self-supporting entity while operating as a part of Emmanuel. In 2020, the school had 31 teachers and 170 students with an annual income of $880,000. The school also offers an early care and late care program.

By 1972, Emmanuel was assuming all financial obligations and contributing significantly to an outreach ministry for others. Approximately 20 percent of the total budget was being given for outreach beyond the church ministry.

It was evident by 1974 that larger facilities were required. A committee was formed to study the needs of the church. As a result of recessionary indicators in the economy at the time, and perhaps a little pessimism, the possibility of increasing the size of the church plant did not materialize.

Second Building Plan

The membership continued to grow and by 1977, 8 years after the ground-breaking on the first unit, the membership had grown to 687. Another committee was formed to look at needs of the church. This time the outlook was more positive and on May 1, 1977 a Charge Conference was held and approval was given to build the second unit. The cost of the second unit was $507,537. Cobb Construction Company was engaged as the contractor. The seeds that had been planted were now producing great harvests for Emmanuel. Membership continued upward, worship services and Sunday School attendance increased each year as did the financial obligations.

The second plan included:

>   Additional Classrooms
>   Enlarged and Modernized Nursery
>   Enlarged Sanctuary and Permanent Pews
>   New and Enlarged Kitchen
>   Gym/Fellowship Hall

Construction commenced in July 1978 and was completed in January 1980. The building committee for the second unit included the following members:

James Michie	Jan Michie
Doris Hall	Ben Waller, Jr.
Doug Lambert	Ron Moore
Emily Hicks	Fran Bass
Gerald Maynard	Fred McDonald
Carl Bonner	Rev. Ken Burnette
Ed Wilson (Chairman)	Bill McLaughlin
D. R. Braswell	Jerry Deaton
Armie Haines	Alan Reiners
Don Pallin	George Long
Olin Adkins	

Copies of the second unit plans are on the following pages.

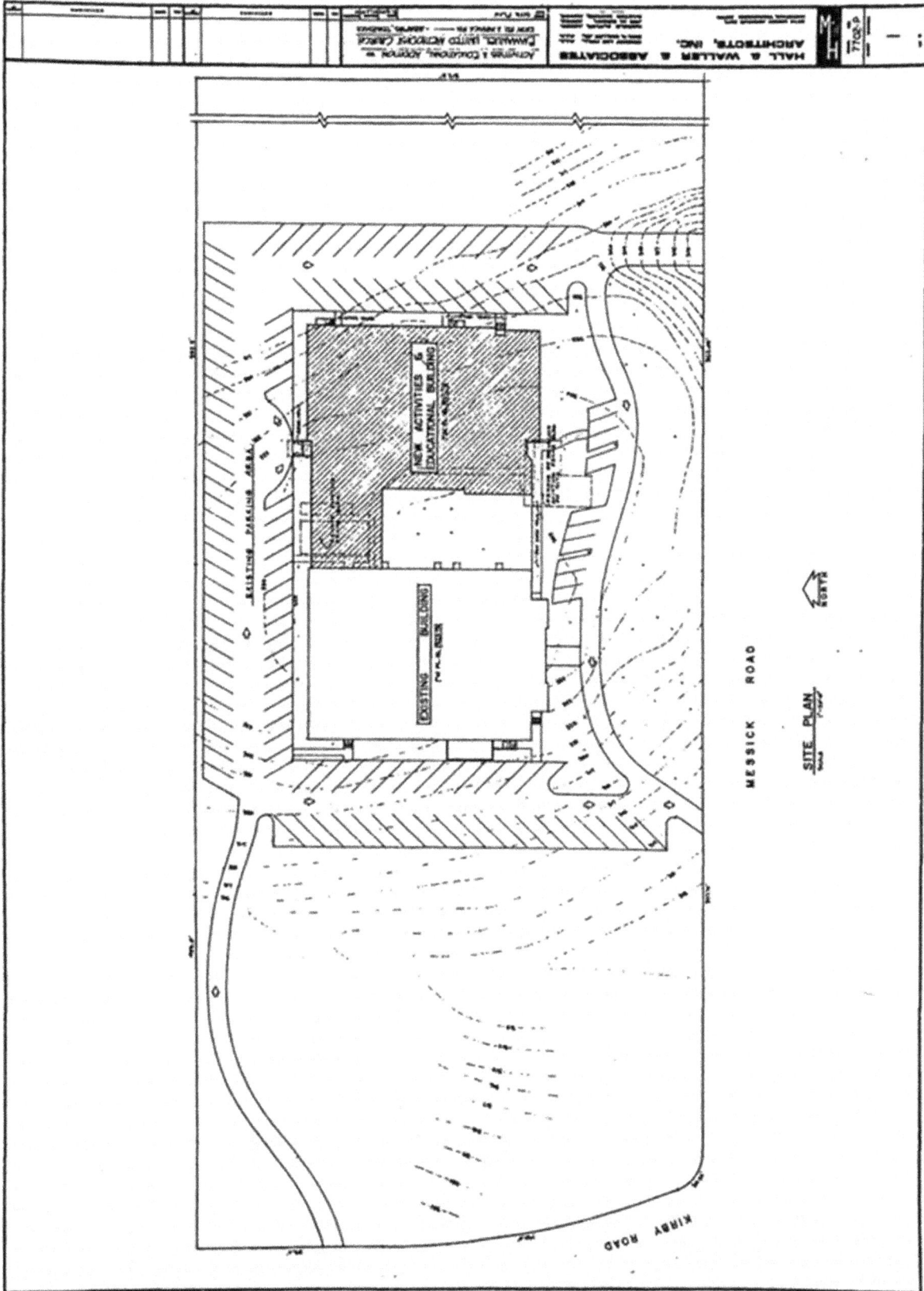

Second Building Plan Elevations

Second Building Plan Elevations

Second Building Plan Elevations

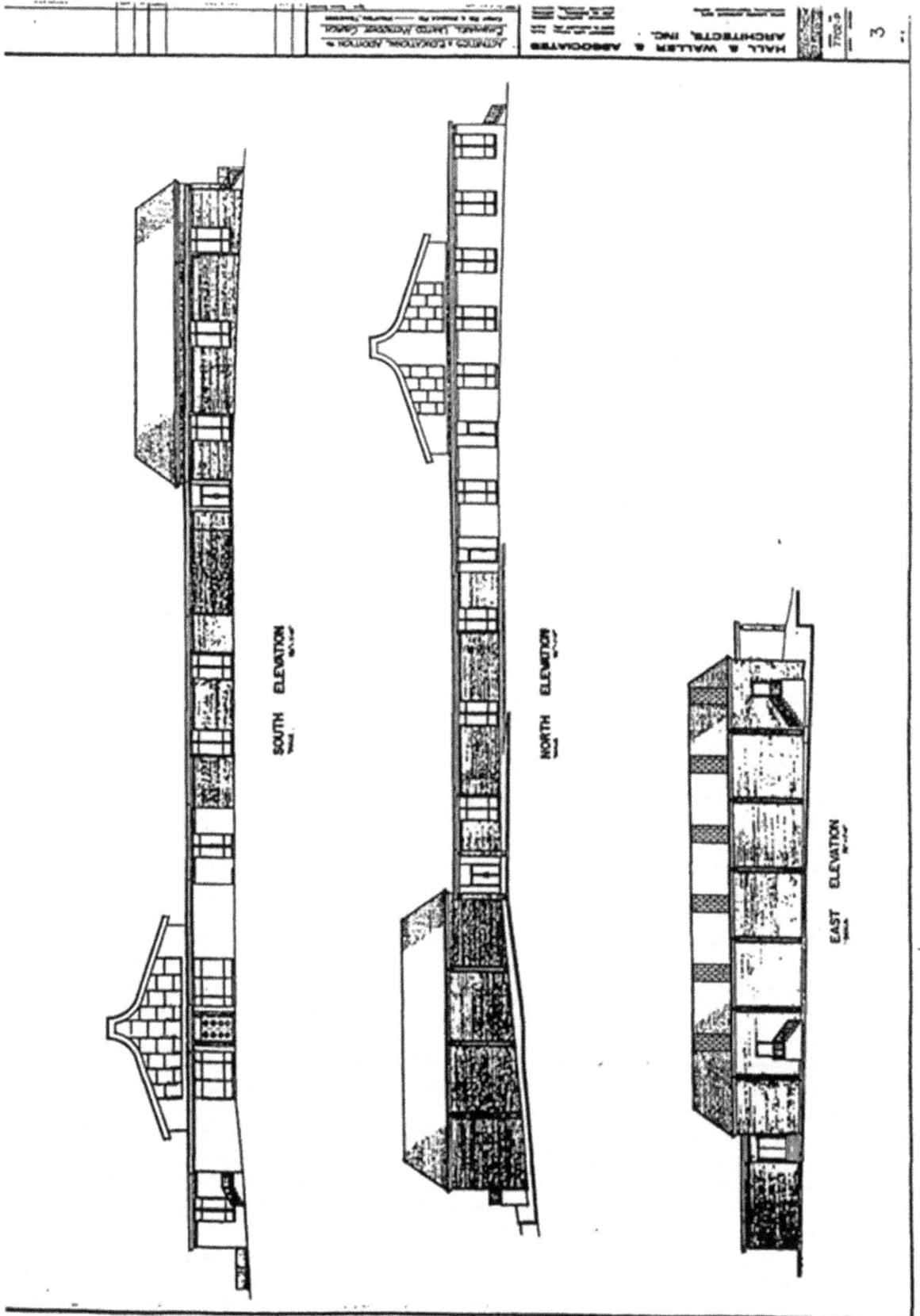

Second Building Plan Elevations

Rev. Harold Watkins

Rev. Ken Burnette had served Emmanuel faithfully for 13 years. The time had come for his departure and Emmanuel received the appointment of Rev. Harold Watkins and his wife Betty. The church remained stable during the appointment of Rev. Watkins. The additional debt resulting from the construction of the second unit put a strain on the finances. Changes often result upon the movement of a minister. Sometimes the change is positive and other times the change is negative.

EMMANUEL UNITED METHODIST CHURCH
Memphis, Tennessee

ORGAN DEDICATION AND RECITAL
April 4, 1982 — 5:00 PM

JAMES A. BRINSON
Guest Organist

Organ Dedication

EMMANUEL UNITED METHODIST CHURCH

Organ Dedication and Recital

Since before the dawn of recorded history wind-blown pipes have been a part of man's sacred and secular ceremonies. When the pipes were placed on a chest and a keyboard added to control the supply of wind to each pipe, the pipe organ was born.

The modern pipe organ usually has two or more keyboards plus a foot-operated pedal-board. Each keyboard controls one division of the entire organ, while each key controls one or more pipes within that division. The pipes themselves, which are either housed in wooden cases or placed in chambers, are made of zinc, copper, tin, lead and wood. Some are of the "whistle" variety, and the remainder are of the "party horn" type. Some divisions of the organ are placed behind Venetian shutters which may be opened and closed to vary the volume.

The organist produces a desired sound by pulling out selected "stops". They are called stops because when they are in the off position, they stop certain sets or "ranks" of pipes from sounding.

The new organ at Emmanuel has ten ranks of pipes divided among two keyboards and pedal. As contributions to the organ fund permit, it is hoped that the organ's full complement of twenty-three ranks can be realized.

Our organ was built in 1964 by the Wicks Organ Company for the Monastery of St. Claire in Evansville, Indiana. Due to the construction of a new and smaller monastery in 1981, this organ became available to Emmanuel.

The Wicks Organ Company had its origins in the early 1900's when three Wick brothers were persuaded by a local priest to try their hand at constructing an organ for St. Paul's Church in Highland, Illinois. This first attempt proved so successful, the Wick brothers built several more organs and by 1906 formed a corporation for organ building and called it the Wicks Organ Company.

Their early instruments all had mechanical action, which means that the valves admitting air to blow the pipes were controlled by levers and rods connected directly to the keys. By 1914 an all electric action had been developed, which proved to be the prototype for today's "DIRECT-ELECTRIC" action. This action was trademarked in 1922 and has been used by Wicks ever since. In this system, the movement of the key closes an electrical contact, and the valves under the pipes are opened by electricity.

Installation of the organ at Emmanuel was done by R. G. Capra Organs, Inc., under the direction of Bob Capra, Southern Director, Wicks Organ Company. Mr. Stanley Sherman has been in charge of day to day installation, and has been assisted by Mr. Bill Hugo. Tonal finishing was done by Mr. Bob Capra and Mr. Dan Nealon. A special thanks to Mr. Ben Waller, architect, Mr. Fred McDonald, for site preparation and Mr. Armie Haines for electrical work.

+ + + + +

Emmanuel United Methodist Church gratefully thanks those who have contributed to the Pipe Organ Fund. Others who wish to make a contribution, either as a gift or as a Memorial, may place their gifts in the offering plates located at the back of the sanctuary, or mail a check to the church office. Your support is greatly appreciated.

Organ Dedication

SERVICE OF DEDICATION FOR THE ORGAN

April 4, 1982

5:00 P.M.

CALL TO WORSHIP   Rev. Harold E. Watkins
Minister: Surely the Lord is in this place.
People: This is none other but the house of God, and this is the gate of heaven.
Minister: Enter into his gates with thanksgiving, and into his courts with praise.
People: O magnify the Lord with me, and let us exalt his name together. Amen.

HYMN   "God of Our Fathers"   No. 552
Janet Templeton, Organist

INVOCATION   Rev. Ken Burnette

ACT OF PRESENTATION   Mr. James Springfield
We present this organ to be dedicated to the glory of Almighty God and for service in this church.

ACT OF DEDICATION   Rev. Harold E. Watkins
In the name of the Father, and of the Son, and of the Holy Spirit, we dedicate this organ to the praise of Almighty God.

We dedicate this organ to the cultivation of a high art: to the interpretation of the message of the masters of music, to an appreciation of the great doxologies of the Church, and to the development of the language of praise which belongeth both to earth and to heaven.

Praise him with stringed instruments and organs. Let everything that hath breath praise the Lord. Praise ye the Lord.

We dedicate this organ to the wedding march, to thanksgiving on festal occasions, and to such inspiration in the service of song that all people may praise the Lord.

O sing unto the Lord a new song: sing unto the Lord, all the earth, in psalms and hymns and spiritual songs, singing and making melody in your heart to the Lord.

We dedicate this organ to the healing of life's discords, and the revealing of the hidden soul of harmony; to the lifting of the depressed and the comforting of the sorrowing; to the humbling of the heart before the eternal mysteries, and the lifting of the soul to abiding beauty and joy, by the gospel of infinite love and good will.

That at the name of Jesus every knee should bow, of things in heaven, and things in earth, and things under the earth; and that every tongue should confess that Jesus Christ is Lord, to the glory of God the Father.

DEDICATION RECITAL

James A. Brinson, Organist

Allegro from "Water Music"   G. F. Handel

Organ Compositions based on hymn tunes
Jesu, Joy of Man's Desiring   J. S. Bach
St. Anne   T. Stuart Archer
Passion Chorale   Johannes Brahms
Now Thank We All Our God   Herbert Grieb

Arabesque   Louis Vierne

Sonata XXIII and XXIV   Domenico Scarlatti

Pastorale   Cesar Franck

Rhumba   Robert Elmore

*BENEDICTION   Rev. Lowell Council

Mr. Brinson is Organist-Choirmaster at Church of the Holy Communion in Memphis. He is a native of Birmingham, Alabama, is married and has two sons, ages 3½ and 1½. He received his Bachelor of Music degree from Southwestern at Memphis in 1970, and holds a Master of Sacred Music degree from Union Theological Seminary in New York City. Before coming to Memphis, he served as Organist-Choirmaster of St. Paul's Episcopal Church in Winter Haven, Florida. While living there, he taught music history, organ and harpsichord at Florida Southern College in Lakeland, and was director for their recital/evensong series. The congregation of Emmanuel would like to express its sincere thanks to Mr. Brinson for serving as a consultant to the Organ Committee in the acquisition of this organ.

Everyone is cordially invited to attend a reception immediately following the recital in the Prime Time Room hosted by the Chancel Choir.

Organ Dedication

THE SPECIFICATIONS OF THE ORGAN

GREAT

8' Principal	61 Pipes
8' Gedeckt (Wood)	61 Pipes
8' Dulciana	61 Pipes
4' Prestant	12 Pipes
4' Dulcet	12 Pipes
Twelfth	
Fifteenth	12 Pipes
Chimes	21 Notes
Tremolo	

SWELL

8' Rohrflote	61 Pipes
8' Violin	61 Pipes
8' Violin Celeste T.C.	49 Pipes
4' Geigen Principal	61 Pipes
4' Traverse Flute	61 Pipes
2 2/3' Nasard	
2' Harmonic Piccolo	12 Pipes
8' Oboe	61 Pipes

PEDAL

16' Bourdon	32 Pipes
16' Lieblich Gedeckt (Soft Wind)	
8' Diapason (Great)	
8' Bass Flute	12 Pipes
8' Dulciana (Great)	
5 1/3' Quint (Swell)	
4' Geigen Diapason (Swell)	
8' Oboe (Swell)	

COUPLERS

Great to Pedal 8'	Swell to Swell 16'
Great to Pedal 4'	Swell Unison
Swell to Pedal 8'	Swell to Swell 4'
Swell to Pedal 4'	Great to Great 16'
Swell to Great 16'	Great Unison
Swell to Great 8'	Great to Great 4'
Swell to Great 4'	

+ + + + +

The members of the Pipe Organ Committee and the congregation of Emmanuel wish to express their deepest gratitude to Mr. James Springfield whose unselfish and untiring efforts made the dream of this magnificent instrument a reality.

Organ Dedication

Dr. Dave Hilliard

Dr. Dave Hilliard was appointed to Emmanuel by the conference in June 1986. His wife, Patsy, daughter, Holly, and son, Hank, would join him to become Emmanuel's third minister. The membership had grown to 1,177 by the end of 1985, with an average worship attendance of 319. With him came a new spirit, greater enthusiasm and a work ethic that would force Emmanuel to be more aggressive in the total program of the church.

Long Range Planning Committee

In May 1987, Emmanuel engaged Rev. Ray Branton, a church consultant, to analyze the programs, worship services, over-all visibility of the church within the community, the church plant and availability of parking.

Emmanuel's second Long Range Planning Committee was formed in July 1989. Included in this committee were:

Dr. Dave Hilliard	Rev. Greg Wilkerson
Ben Waller, Jr.	Alan Humphreys
Dr. Jerry Deaton	Dick Barton
Durrell Dallas	John Bumpers
Sandra Newsome	Glenn Hopper
Bill McLaughlin	Charles Dyott
Frances McDonald	David Frye
Sandy Eggers	Don Keeney
Karen Clark	David Zanka

The objective of the committee was to develop a three-to-five-year plan for the church programs and facilities. The committee was broken down into sub-groups, from July to October 1989, that studied eight different identified areas of need. A preliminary report was then prepared and forwarded to Rev. Branton, the consultant, as he was already familiar with Emmanuel and its programs.

Listed below are the major recommendations made by the consultant after reviewing the work of the sub-committees:

- More Sunday School Classes.
- Expansion and better utilization of the sanctuary.
- Substantial increase in nursery space and facility.
- A more functional physical plan for the administrative area which would afford better communications between staff personnel.
- More effective use of computer equipment.
- The purchase of a church bus.

The long-range planning committee accepted the consultant's report and continued their analysis of the recommendations through July 1990. It was at this time, that this committee made its recommendation to the Administrative Council, which adapted and implemented most of the recommendations of the consultant.

The committee also recommended to the Administrative Council that a building committee be formed. The committee also recommended that the building committee, when appointed, study the findings of the long-range planning committee and the consultant and if their conclusions were in agreement, move forward to develop a detailed specification of requirements which satisfied the identified needs of the church. The committee also recommended that the building committee work with the stewardship and finance committees to develop a campaign to fund such a building program.

Building Committee

On July 22, 1990, a Building Committee was formed. Subsequently, Ben Waller, Jr. was engaged as the Church's architect and given permission to prepare preliminary plans and estimates for a facility that would accommodate the needs as discussed herein above.

Upon completion of the preliminary drawings by the architect, the building committee began meetings to study the plans and make recommendations for possible changes. This process continued until early 1991. The final plans, when completed, reflected changes in the areas as follows:

• A new administrative/education building to contain approximately 16,500 square feet and be constructed on the west side of the Church. There would be four adult classrooms, administrative offices, library/conference room, choir room, robe rooms, hand-bell choir room, children's choir room and restrooms on the main level.

• The lower level to consist of six adult classrooms, a scout room or storage room, and restrooms.

• The sanctuary expansion and renovation to include enlargement of the choir loft to accommodate sixty-eight people. The organ to be upgraded to its maximum level, the sanctuary to be expanded to seat an additional one hundred-sixty people, and the vestibule to be enlarged to three times the present size.

• Some adult classrooms to be converted to children's classrooms. Existing administrative offices to become parlor which may double as a classroom. In addition, the nursery to be expanded and modernized.

On April 1, 1991, the Building Committee made the following recommendations to the Administrative Council/Charge Conference:

"That Emmanuel under-take a building campaign of $1,521,742 to construct a new Administrative/ Education/Music Building, to renovate portions of the present administrative and education space for better use and to expand and partially renovate the present sanctuary.

"The committee further recommended that the professional church fund raising firm of Resource Services, Inc. of Dallas, Texas be employed by Emmanuel to assist in raising the money needed for such a building program and that Emmanuel enter into a contract in the amount of $43,000 for their services.

"The committee further recognized that the actions taken were subject to the approval of the congregation and Charge Conference."

The Church Conference was held on Sunday, May 5, 1991, and the recommendation as outlined above were approved for the New Administrative and Educational Building.

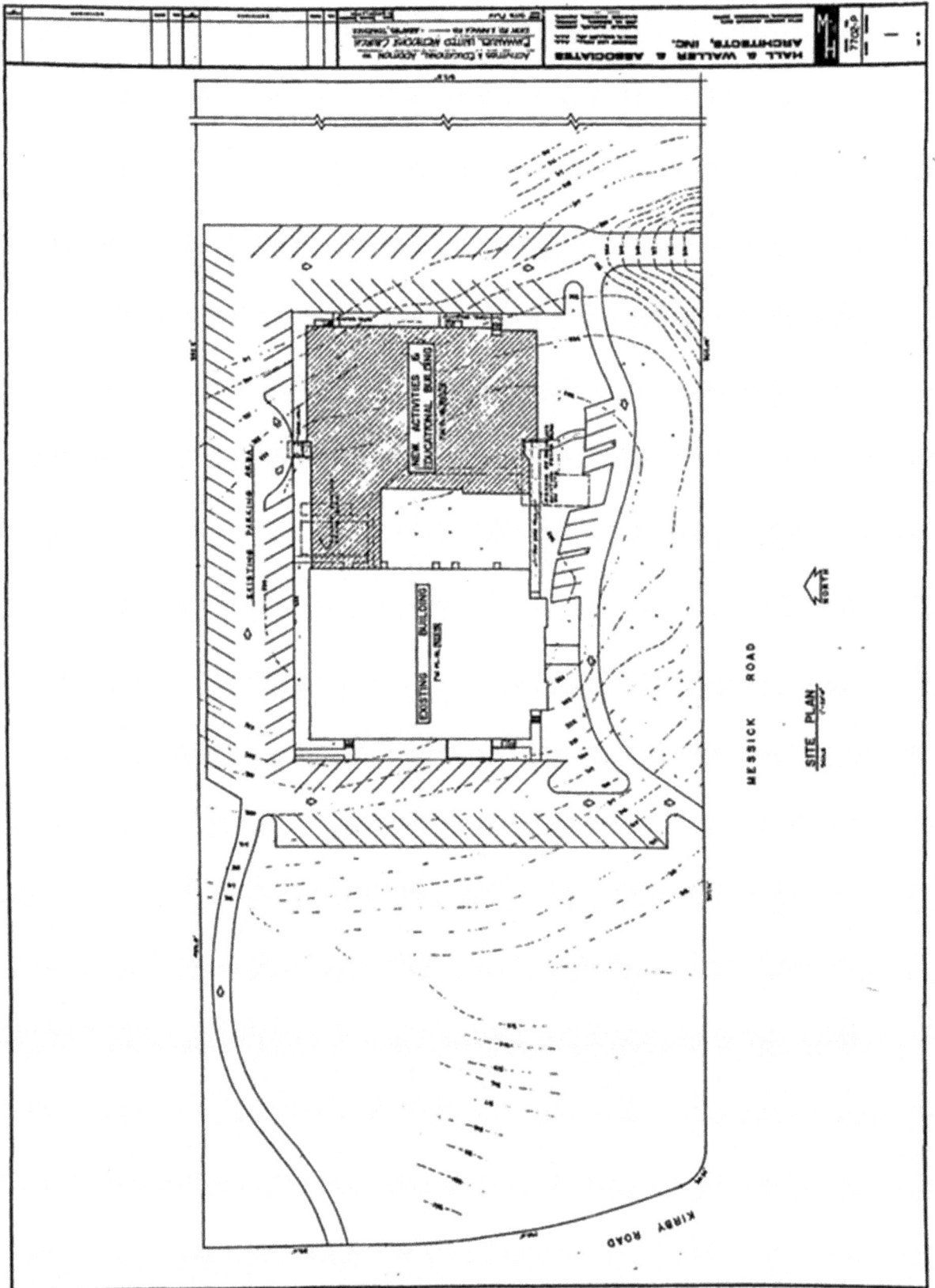

Education Building Plan

Education Building Plan

The following costs were assigned to the new facility:

Upper Level-$505,500 ($50.00/sq. ft.)
Lower Level-$384,000 ($60.00/sq. ft.)
$889,500
Renovation of existing areas of
Present offices, classrooms,
library to make new classrooms,
nursery room, parlor and corridor

Parlor	18,000
Nursery	30,000
Corridor and Classrooms	12,000
	$60,000

Paving, Site Development	46,400
Landscaping and irrigation	15,000
	$61,400

Organ Expansion	
(From 10 to 30 ranks)	55,000
Furnishings	16,000
Architectural Fee	61,797
RSI Fund Raising	43,000
Promotional	10,000
Misc. Expenses Appraisal, Lender Points	
Interest, Insurance, etc.)	100,000
	$285,797

Sanctuary Renovation	
($75/sq. ft. – Includes Pews)	90,000
Narthex and Storage Areas	93,765
Choir Loft and Chancel Area	41,280
	$225,045
Grand Total	$1,521,742

As outlined previously, expansion of the choir loft and chancel area, sanctuary and narthex were included in this phase of construction. Pictures showing part of the expansion is included with additional photographs at the end of the transcript.

Dr. Jerry Deaton and Clyde Moore were chosen as co-directors of the financial campaign. During the months of June through August 1991, committees were busy at their assigned tasks working toward victory Sunday which was scheduled for October 6, 1991.

Perhaps it should be mentioned that three goals were established in the financial campaign as follows:

- Launch Goal $600,000
- Challenge Goal $1,000,000
- Celebration Goal $1,300,000

On Victory Sunday, pledges in excess of $1,730,000 had been made to be repaid over a three-year period. The theme of the financial campaign was "Faith in Action". Certainly, faith was demonstrated in this campaign.

The new facilities were completed in 1993. At the end of the pledge period, sufficient funds had been received to not only pay off the construction loan for the new addition, but the total debt of the church.

Few churches, with a plant the size of Emmanuel, could boast of being debt free, with reserves established for emergencies.

As time passed, the traditional thoughts of a church needing a parsonage changed. The feeling was that the pastoral family could benefit from owning their own home, building equity for future investment or retirement. The church parsonage, acquired in 1968 for its first minister, was acquired by the Hilliards.

Education and evangelism have always been priorities of Emmanuel. During the years of Dr. Hilliard, a lot of emphasis was placed in these areas. One of the long-lasting studies was the Disciples, which lasted over twenty years. Dr. Hilliard taught the first class. Dr. Jerry Deaton and his wife Nancy Jo stepped up and led the Disciple classes for several years. Other studies followed, including Jesus In The Gospels and Gospel Parallels. Dr. Wayne Hamm was instrumental in promoting these and other studies. Dr. Hilliard was appointed District Superintendent in June 1995 after nine years at Emmanuel.

CELEBRATING

EMMANUEL

1968 - 1993

25 Years

OUR
SILVER
ANNIVERSARY

June 6, 1993

Emmanuel United Methodist Church

CELEBRATION OF THE FUTURE   A Challenge
Scripture: I John 2:28-3:2
read by Mrs. Mary Lewis Butler, Chairperson, *Administrative Council*
Mr. Bob Baker, representative of our newer members
Dr. David M. Hilliard, Jr.   Senior Minister
Anthem: "All Creatures of Our God and King   arr. Rutter
Chancel Choir and Cross Notes
(Congregation is invited to sing on the last verse)

*RECESSIONAL HYMN: "I Love Thy Kingdom, Lord"   No. 540

BALLOON CELEBRATION   on the front and west parking lot

BENEDICTION   "Blest Be the Tie That Binds"

RECEPTION in the Gym

✝ ✝ ✝ ✝ ✝ ✝

OUR CHURCH THIS WEEK

SUNDAY: 2:30 P.M. - Joint Choir Practice of Emmanuel and St. Luke's Choirs
     4:30 P.M. - Wednesday Noon - Annual Conference Jackson, TN Civic Center
MONDAY: 7:00 P.M. - Men's Softball: Houston Levee Field, #3
     5:30 P.M. - Covenant Discipleship Group
TUESDAY: 7:00 P.M. - Women's Fifth Tradition (AA)
WEDNESDAY: 7:00 P.M. - Marketplace 29 AD volunteers: Friendship rm.
     6:45 P.M. - "Process" Group: 50-Something room
     7:30 P.M. - Chancel Choir rehearses
THURSDAY: 6:45 A.M. - Men's Prayer Group: Youth Lounge
     7:00 P.M. - Lay Involvement in Worship Committee
SUNDAY: 6:00 P.M. - Membership Committee meets

The Flowers on the Altar are given by Juanna and Bill Phillips in memory of Robin, Rachael, and Justin Phillips.

The Flowers in the Foyer are given by Sarah Lee Pilley, sister of Virginia Barnette, in loving memory of their mother, Margaret S. Pigue.

Last Day to Register for Vacation Bible School. Forms are available in the Sunday School class rooms or in the narthex.

This is the Last Day to place your T-shirt order with the Genesis Sunday School Class in order to receive them before Market Place 29 AD.

Silver Anniversary

CELEBRATION!
In Observance of the 25th Anniversary of
EMMANUEL UNITED METHODIST CHURCH
June 6, 1993

WELCOME   Mr. Bill McLaughlin
Chair, 25th Anniversary Committee

PRELUDE: "Lord You Give the Great Commission"   arr. Lovelace
(#584, please note the words)

CALL TO WORSHIP:
Leader: Unless the Lord builds the house,
PEOPLE: THOSE WHO BUILD IT LABOR IN VAIN.
Leader: Unless the Lord guards the city
PEOPLE: THE GUARD KEEPS WATCH IN VAIN.
(Ps. 127:1)

INVOCATION: (in unison)
O God, our help in ages past, our hope for years to come, our shelter from the stormy blast, and our eternal home! Stand in this modern hallowed place of worship and study as you stood in the Holy of Holies in the ancient Temple. Fill us with Your love and send us forth in Your power. In the name of Jesus Christ our Lord. Amen.

*PROCESSIONAL HYMN: "God of Grace and God of Glory"   No. 577
*APOSTLES' CREED   No. 881
*GLORIA PATRI

CELEBRATING THE PAST
Scripture: Our History
Acts 2:38-47
read by Miss Sarah Little

Rev. Ken Burnette, founding pastor: 1968-1981   Pastor, Mullins UMC
Mrs. Nelle Waller, Charter member, 1968-present
Director, Emmanuel Kindergarten

Anthem: "The Church's One Foundation"   arr. Manz
Chancel Choir

CELEBRATING THE PRESENT   Consecrating and Reconsecrating the Building

Declaration of Purpose   Rev. Greg Wilkerson
Presentation of the Buildings:
Mr. Dick Barton, Building Committee Chairperson

Prayers of Consecration   Rev. Greg Wilkerson
Dr. Jerry Deaton, "Faith in Action" Campaign Co-Chairperson
Mr. Clyde Moore, "Faith in Action" Campaign Co-Chairperson
Mrs. Jane Johnston, Board of Trustees Chairperson
Dr. Tony Powers, Emmanuel Lay Leader/Chair of Staff-Lay Council
Mr. David Zanca, Committee on Finance Chairperson
Mr. Ben Waller, Jr., Chief Architect and Charter Member of Emmanuel

(The congregation is asked to respond at the following places in the Prayers of Consecration)

Mrs. Jane Johnston: ....In the name of the Father, and of the Son, and of the Holy Spirit,
PEOPLE: WE CONSECRATE THIS BUILDING.
Dr. Tony Powers: To the spiritual enrichment of all who shall come here seeking knowledge, in the name of the Father, and of the Son, and of the Holy Spirit,
PEOPLE: WE CONSECRATE THIS BUILDING.
Mr. David Zanca: To the loyal service of those whose training and devotion have prepared them to lead students toward the truth, in the name of the Father, and of the Son, and of the Holy Spirit,
PEOPLE: WE CONSECRATE THIS BUILDING.
Mr. Ben Waller, Jr.:   To that ministry of administration upon whose ability and faithfulness depends the wise conduct of our life together and our ministry in the world, in the name of the Father, and of the Son, and of the Holy Spirit,
PEOPLE: WE CONSECRATE THIS BUILDING. AND WE CONSECRATE OURSELVES ANEW TO THAT SERVICE OF HUMANITY IN WHICH WE PERFORM THE TRUE SERVICE OF GOD.

Closing Prayer: Rev. Greg Wilkerson
Reception of Our Tithes and Offerings
Anthem: "Prayer of Consecration"
*Presentation of Our Gifts/Doxology

Incorporation of Church in 1993

Like all entities, risk is a consideration for all those involved in church related activities. In an effort to minimize the risk, the Church was incorporated in the name of Emmanuel United Methodist Church, Inc. on August 18, 1993.

Incorporation of Church in 1993

MINUTES OF THE ORGANIZATION MEETING OF
THE DIRECTORS OF EMMANUEL UNITED METHODIST CHURCH, INC.
September 12, 1993

The former Board of Trustees of Emmanuel United Methodist Church, having been named in the Charter of Emmanuel United Methodist Church-Memphis, Inc. as the initial Directors thereof, do hereby and by these presents act as authorized in the Tennessee Nonprofit Corporation Act for the purposes of organizing the Corporation and transacting such business as may be incidental thereto as required by the Act. To the end that the Corporation be organized for the purpose of commencing business, the following resolutions are hereby adopted by and on behalf of the Corporation:

RESOLVED, that the Charter of Emmanuel United Methodist Church-Memphis, Inc., together with the Certificate of the Secretary of State attached hereto, as filed on the 19th day of August, 1993, in the Office of the Secretary of State of the State of Tennessee, and as recorded with the Register of Shelby County, Tennessee, as Instrument Number DU9471, be and the same are hereby approved and ordered to be filed as part of the permanent record of the Corporation;

FURTHER RESOLVED, that the document attached hereto entitled "Bylaws of Emmanuel United Methodist Church-Memphis, Inc." executed by the President, be and the same is hereby adopted as the Bylaws for the government of the Corporation and its affairs subject, however, to the right of the Board of Directors of the Corporation to amend or repeal the same or to adopt new bylaws;

FURTHER RESOLVED, that the acts of James D. Wilson in incorporating the Corporation are hereby ratified and adopted, and further that his resignation as Incorporator, dated August 31, 1993, is hereby accepted;

FURTHER RESOLVED, that pursuant to the Bylaws, the following persons be and they are hereby elected as officers of the Corporation, each to hold office for a term of one year or until his successor shall have been duly elected:

President:	Jane Johnston
Vice President:	Joe Spicer
Secretary:	Chris Armstrong
Treasurer:	Chris Armstrong

The foregoing actions are taken on this the 12 day of SEPTEMBER, 1993

Jane P. Johnston
Director   PRES.

Director   SECRETARY

Mark Lange
Director

Joe J. Borge
Director

Walter M. Compton
Director

Pat Sharkey
Director

Mary Lane Buth
Director

Richard G. Swebe
Director

Director

BYLAWS OF
EMMANUEL UNITED METHODIST CHURCH, INC.

A Tennessee Nonprofit Corporation

Article I
Purposes

The purposes for which this nonprofit corporation is organized are to serve any objectives of the Emmanuel United Methodist Church prescribed by The Book of Discipline of The United Methodist Church [hereinafter "The Book of Discipline"], including but not limited to all charitable, educational or religious undertakings, purposes, programs and projects of said Church and to maintain in perpetual duration and succession an Emmanuel United Methodist Church, whether at its present location or elsewhere, and to continue the vitality of the Church by and through the grace of Jesus Christ.

Article II
Board of Directors

1.   Membership on the Board. The initial membership of the Board of Directors shall be comprised of the members of the Board of Trustees in office at the time of incorporation.   Once incorporation takes place, the Board of Trustees shall automatically assume the role of the Board of Directors. The board members shall serve without compensation but shall be reimbursed for reasonable expenses incurred on behalf of the Corporation. The board members shall have no personal liability for the Corporation except for misfeance in office.

2.   Election to the Board. When a board member's term is up, a new member shall be elected in same manner that The Book of Discipline sets forth for the election of Board of Trustee members. The new members of the Board of Directors shall be nominated and voted on in the same manner that The Book of Discipline sets forth for the nomination and election of Board of Trustee members. Further, the same group of persons given, in The Book of Discipline, the duty of electing the Board of Trustee members shall elect the Board of Directors of the Corporation.

3.   Officers of the Board. The Board of Directors shall elect from the membership thereof to hold office for a term of one year, or until their successors shall be elected, a president, vice president, and secretary, and if need requires, a treasurer. However, the offices of president and secretary shall not be held by the same person. The secretary shall be responsible for preparing minutes of the Board of Directors' meetings and for authenticating records of the corporation and for keeping the minute book in order. Also, the president shall be a member of the Emmanuel United Methodist Church. The duties of each officer shall be the same as are generally connected with the office held and which are usually and commonly discharged by the holder thereof.

4.   Procedures.   All procedures outlined in The Book of Discipline as applicable to a Board of Trustees shall be the official procedures of the Board of Directors of the Corporation. The procedures from The Book of Discipline that are to apply to the Board of Directors shall include, but are not limited to, those procedures relating to meetings and quorum.

5.   Powers and Duties of the Board.   The Board of Directors shall have the same powers and duties as those delegated by The Book of Discipline to Boards of Trustees. The scope of the powers and duties of the Board of Directors is explicitly limited to the scope of the Board of Trustee's powers and duties, as set forth in The Book of Discipline. The Board of Directors shall not attempt to assume or abrogate any powers or duties given by The Book of Discipline to any other church group, committee, or board. All corporate powers other than those delegated by the Book of Discipline to the Board of Trustees shall be exercised by the Administrative Council of Emmanuel United Methodist Church pursuant to the Book of Discipline.

Article III
Corporate Property

The title to all property now owned or hereafter acquired by Emmanuel United Methodist Church, and any organization, board, commission, society, or similar body connected therewith shall be held by and/or conveyed to the corporate body in its corporate name in trust for the use and benefit of the local church corporation and of the United Methodist Church. Every instrument of conveyance of real estate shall contain the appropriate trust clause as set forth in ¶2503 of The Book of Discipline.

Article IV
Fiscal Year

The fiscal year of the Corporation shall begin on the 1st day of January and end on the 31st day of December in each year.

Article V
Amendments

These By-Laws may be altered, amended or repealed and new By-Laws may be adopted by the Board at any regular or special meeting of the Board.

Article VI
Dissolution

If this Corporation is dissolved by the Board of Directors and if the congregation forms a successor unincorporated church, then, upon dissolution, all the property and interest of the Corporation shall be distributed to a Board of Trustees, elected by the Charge Conference of the said successor Emmanuel United Methodist Church, which shall supervise, oversee, and care for all such property. If no such successor church is formed, however, then the remaining assets and property of the Corporation shall be distributed to such entity or entities selected according to ¶2548 of The Book of Discipline.

Article VII
The Book of Discipline

The provisions contained in The Book of Discipline are hereby incorporated into the By-Laws of this Corporation. Further, if there is a conflict between any of the explicitly enunciated By-Laws set forth herein and any of The Book of Discipline provisions, then The Book of Discipline provisions shall control.

CERTIFICATION

I certify that the foregoing is an exact copy of the By-Laws of Emmanuel United Methodist Church which were adopted by the Board of Directors on the date noted below.

By: _Jane A. Johnston_
PRESIDENT
Emmanuel United Methodist Church

Date: 9/12/93

Rev. Tommy Edwards

Rev. Tommy Edwards and his wife, Doris, were appointed to Emmanuel in 1995. Rev. Edwards was Emmanuel's fourth minister and Emmanuel would be Rev. Edwards' last appointment. The Faith In Action Campaign had been very successful and Rev. Edwards arrived at Emmanuel when the church was in a debt free position. Rev. Edwards retired in 2001 after serving Emmanuel six years.

Rev. Barry Henson

Upon the retirement of Rev. Tommy Edwards, Rev. Barry Henson was appointed by the conference to serve at Emmanuel. Rev. Henson and his wife, Selena, would serve as Emmanuel's pastoral family for six years and part of a seventh year.

His interest in the great history of Emmanuel, led to the establishment of a History and Archives Department. In March 2004, an attempt was made to establish an Archives Department of the church. Unfortunately, there had been little previous interest in preserving the history of Emmanuel. Some of the artifacts were accidentally destroyed when planning for a new building program. It was and continues to be difficult to pull together some of the early pictures, documents, etc. relating to the church's history.

Notwithstanding this, effort has been made to gather and preserve Emmanuel's history.

Property Purchase

As in everything, time brings on changes and new challenges. In 1967, when the property was purchased to construct a new church to become Emmanuel, the 5.24 acres appeared sufficient for the needs of the church. However, as time passed and the church grew, it was evident that Emmanuel's growth and future development would be contained unless additional property could be purchased.

Contact was made with the owner, James Ellis, of the property on the south side of Messick Road, but purchasing the property was not possible. Due to the configuration of the land, eastward movement appeared to be the only opportunity.

Contact had been made with David Martin and his wife who owned the property that was adjacent to the east property line of Emmanuel. Initial contact had resulted in the Martin's having no interest in selling the property. After a couple of years, the Martins contacted the church indicating their interest in divesting themselves of the property. Emmanuel, after much discussion, decided to enter into a contract to purchase the property for $1,500,000. Financing of the property was arranged through a local bank and the sale was consummated.

In 2002, the Church Council approved spending $30,000 to engage Fleming Associates Architects to look in-depth at Emmanuel's existing church plant and acreage to the east of the church. Drawings were prepared for a master plan incorporating the two properties; however the cost was too exorbitant for the church to undertake the building program as outlined by the study.

By this time, Dr. Hilliard had retired and had moved back to Memphis. He and Patsy, his wife, never wanted to leave Emmanuel and in fact maintained their personal home on Messick Road while he was serving as district superintendent in Kentucky. Dave and Patsy moved back into their home on Messick Road and were once again included in the congregation of Emmanuel.

Upon the purchase of the Martin property, Dr. Hilliard was elected to lead a capital campaign to pay for the purchase of the property. The campaign theme was "Secure The Future."

The budget during the years that Rev. Henson was minister grew from $990,000 to $1,439,537. One real positive for Emmanuel was that it had always been able to meet financial obligations as scheduled. In the church's history there has never been a year when conference givings were not met.

Emmanuel has always been known as one of the stronger churches in the conference. In 2007, Emmanuel was again called upon to supply the need for a district superintendent. Due to other changes in the conference, the bishop had to appoint a district superintendent during mid-year and Rev. Henson was elected to fill that position.

Rev. Larry Daniel

Rev. Larry Daniel was appointed in September 2007 to fill the vacancy of Rev. Henson who was appointed district superintendent. Rev. Daniel and his wife, Marilyn, arrived at Emmanuel when it was at its highest point since 1995.

In 2007, dialog began between Emmanuel and Oakhaven United Methodist Church with regard to merging. Several members of Emmanuel were once members of Oakhaven. Also, Dr. Hilliard and Dr. Daniel had served as pastors of Oakhaven in previous years. Oakhaven's membership and attendance had gradually decreased to a point where it was not economically feasible to continue operating. Upon agreement of both congregations and approval of the conference, the two churches merged in 2007. All assets of Oakhaven moved over to Emmanuel. The real estate was transferred to the balance sheet of Emmanuel, and upon disposition of the property, the funds were moved into a reserve account.

Emmanuel received many of the active members from the Oakhaven congregation. Those that became a part of Emmanuel made a significant contribution in music, education and overall support.

Rev. Daniel started a task force to review what additional building needs Emmanuel might have, especially as related to children's ministry. Rev. Daniel would serve Emmanuel for three and one-half years.

Dr. David Comperry

Dr. David Comperry and his wife, Nancy, were appointed to Emmanuel by the Conference in 2010 to become Emmanuel's senior minister. Dr. Comperry became Emmanuel's seventh minister in its 42-year history. Dr. Comperry was received by Emmanuel from Jackson Northside United Methodist Church. Dr. Comperry and his wife would serve Emmanuel for seven years to June 2017.

Vision

In 2011, a Vision Team was created to faithfully discern the ministry possibilities God was leading and equipping Emmanuel to engage in during the next five to ten years. This would be the first study of its kind in more than twenty-five years. The Vision Team, along with the guidance and direction of Dr. Comperry, tackled many projects. Continued discussions and analysis materialized into a master building plan and new building program.

The Vision Committee consisted of the following members:

Billy Cochran	Dr. David Comperry
Susan Dorian	Mike Fay
Linda Gabriel	Kay Kelly
Jeff McAlexander	Bill McCary
Bill McLaughlin	Bill McWaters
Susie Palmer	Kevin Presley
Andrea Quinn	Susan Schmidt

In 2013, Hord Architects was engaged to look at Emmanuel's current space, programs and needs and make recommendations regarding its future. At the recommendation of the Vision Committee, the Church Council approved a budget of $20,000 to complete the study.

Some of the early considerations and questions in determining the visions of Emmanuel were:

• What does God want?
• What are the current strengths and limitations?
• What needs to be done to be more fruitful?

In response:

• God wants us to be more faithful.
• God wants us to be humble servants.
• God wants us to minister to those we come into contact with daily.

In response:

- Established church in stable neighborhood.
- Debt free church plant.
- Educated and talented congregation and staff.
- Geographical and topographical barriers.
- Commitment/willingness to get involved to extent required.
- Failure or unwillingness to communicate with congregation.

In response:

- A Revival! Enthusiasm! Energy!
- Become more reverent in worship and song.
- Communicate with our congregation.
- Commitment.

Some of the early objectives were:

- Enhance children/youth ministries and increase young adult membership.
- Improve the grounds/landscape to enhance "street" visibility and increase parking. A plan for needed fellowship/event /alternative worship space.

Dr. Wade Cox

Dr. Wade Cox was appointed in July 2017 to be Emmanuel's eighth minister and continues to serve as the Senior Minister. His wife, Susan, son Davis, and daughter Brooke became part of the membership of Emmanuel. He came at a time when Emmanuel was in a significant building program. Dr. Cox brought new enthusiasm and energy which enabled the building program to continue moving forward to completion on budget.

Master Plan

A Master Plan to accommodate all the church's identified needs was prepared by Hord Architects. The first phase of the study was completed, and plans were drawn to meet the projected needs of Emmanuel. Part of the plan was achieved by sacrificing some of the adult classrooms for movement and improvement of the children's department. New classrooms for the children were created. This was accepted with great enthusiasm. Jane Kinzer, the children's coordinator at the time, did a wonderful job in this transition.

The new plan also included a fellowship hall, kitchen, showers in the gym area, two new, large meeting rooms, an enlarged main entrance and an elevator in the two-story area.

In early 2018, the church began to discern the practicality of making this Master Plan a reality. The sale of the property next door generated some initial funding.

Architects then worked with the Vision Team on the first new building in 25 years and a consultant helped develop a Capital Campaign which took place in April/May of 2019.

After a successful campaign and through the action of a charge conference in June of 2019, a building committee was established to plan and implement the construction of a new fellowship hall and kitchen, youth room, community room, food pantry and elevator.

The first phase of the study of Hord Architects was completed and plans were drawn to meet the immediate projected needs of the church

The extra land, east of the church was also incorporated in the study by Hord Architects. Consideration was given to the sale of lots already developed that could be accessed from a street on the north side of the property, to assist in obtaining funds to improve the balance of the property into athletic fields and or other uses.

Subsequently, it was decided that the church was not in the land or subdivision development business, and the decision was made to sell the entire property.

With approval of the purchaser, the church was able to reserve a small part of the property for additional parking.

The Master Plan also included a street-scape project that completely revamped and beautified the view of the church from Messick Road. The street-scape renovation included the removal of trees, planting of new shrubbery, graded, sodded, new trees and a sprinkler system installed. The centerpiece of the street-scape was the installation of a staircase from Messick. There was $3.2 million pledged in addition to $750,000 from the land sale. Gap type financing was arranged through a local bank to cover the additional cost of completion in November of 2021.

With funding from the sale of the eastern most property, the Vision Committee and the Trustees, completed the street-scape project in the fall of 2019.

Part of the street-scape, new signs, and the new building under construction are also included on the pages which follow.

Building Committee Members

Dr. Wade Cox	Rev. Linda Gabriel
Rev. Kevin Presley	Bill McWaters, Chairman
Rand Bouldin	Armie Haines
Carolyn Cochran	Jim Lloyd
Shelia Coleman	Matt Lott
Jimmy Crumpler	Wendell McAlexander
Danny Faulk	Jane Kinzer
Courtney Fussell	Susie Palmer
Libba Fyke	Becca Smith
Terry Glazer	

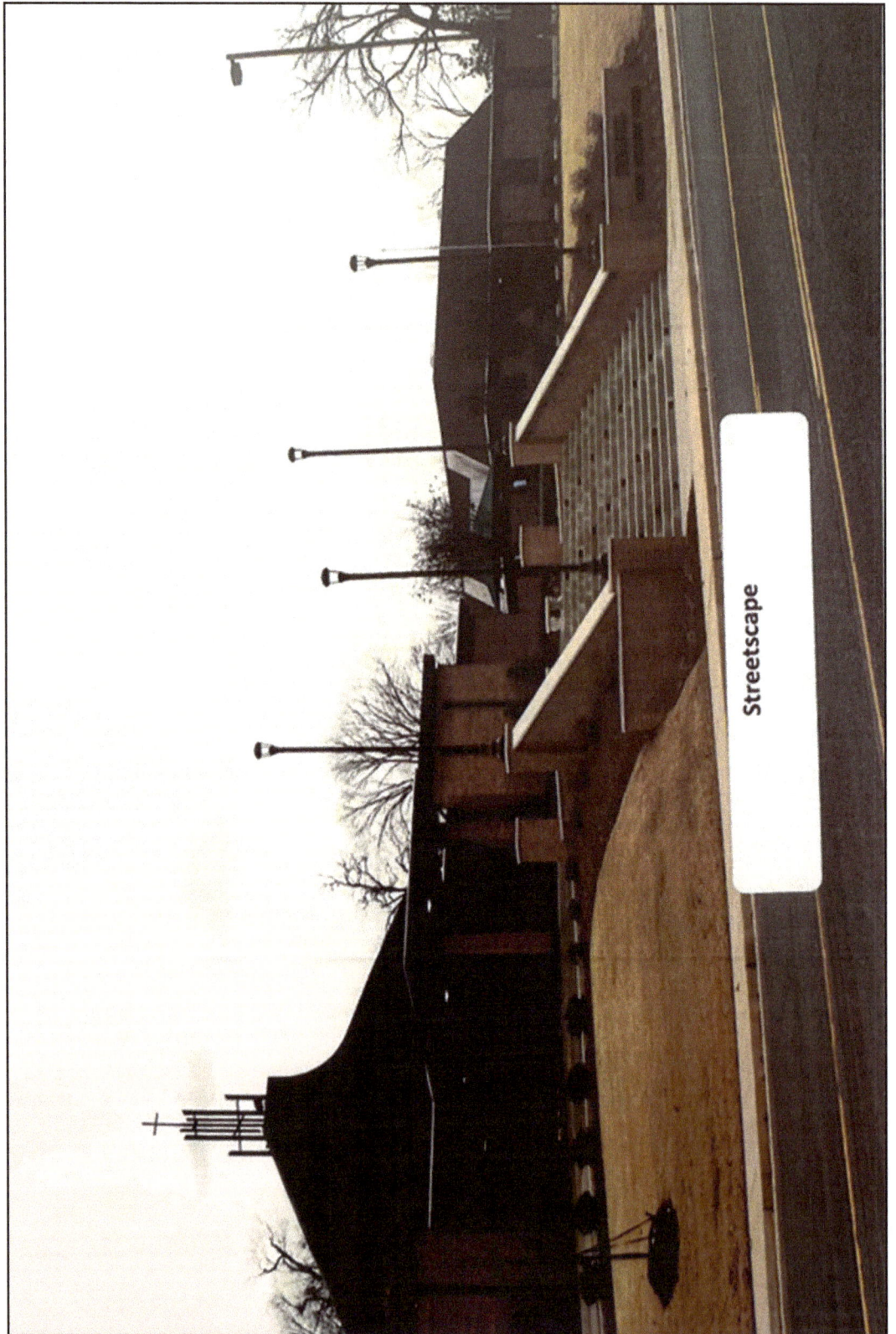

Streetscape

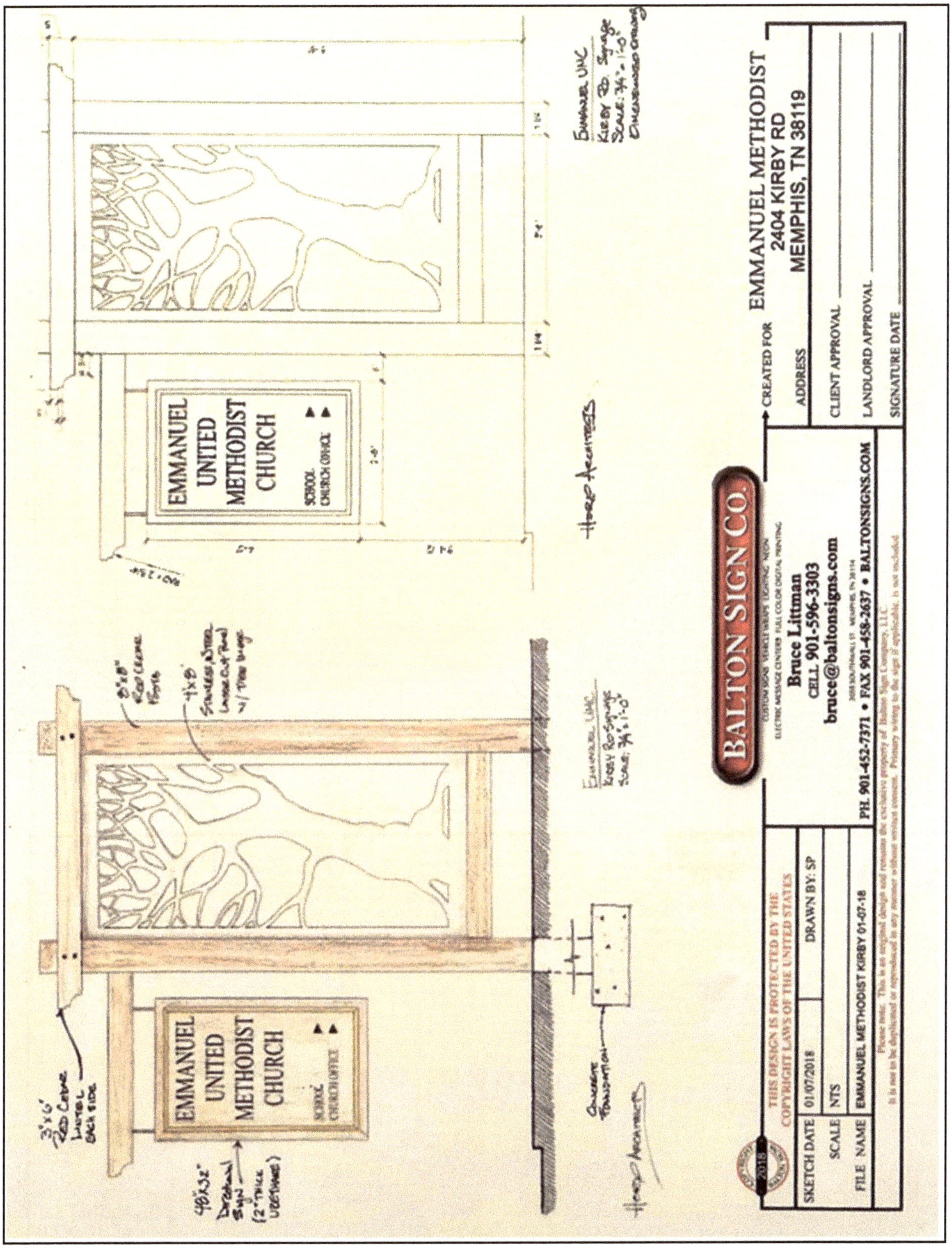

EMMANUEL UNITED METHODIST CHURCH
SCHOOL
CHURCH OFFICE
BALTON SIGN CO.
Bruce Littman
CELL 901-596-3303
bruce@baltonsigns.com
PH. 901-452-7371 • FAX 901-458-2637 • BALTONSIGNS.COM
CREATED FOR EMMANUEL METHODIST
ADDRESS 2404 KIRBY RD MEMPHIS, TN 38119
CLIENT APPROVAL
LANDLORD APPROVAL
SIGNATURE DATE
THIS DESIGN IS PROTECTED BY THE COPYRIGHT LAWS OF THE UNITED STATES
SKETCH DATE 01/07/2018
DRAWN BY: SP
SCALE NTS
FILE NAME EMMANUEL METHODIST KIRBY 01-07-18

EMMANUEL
UNITED METHODIST CHURCH
AND KINDERGARTEN
2404 KIRBY RD

10'-0"

34"

5.62"
4.15"
4.15"
3.25"

SCALE: 1/2" = 1'

MANUFACTURE AND INSTALL
ONE NON-ILLUMINATED DOUBLE SIDED MONUMENT SIGN
WITH DIMENSIONAL LETTERING / LOGO AS PER SPECS

BALTON SIGN CO.

CUSTOM SIGNS · VEHICLE WRAPS · LIGHTING · NEON
ELECTRIC MESSAGE CENTERS · FULL COLOR DIGITAL PRINTING
Bruce Littman
CELL 901-596-3303
bruce@baltonsigns.com

New Church Signs

CREATED FOR   EMMANUEL METHODIST
2404 KIRBY RD
MEMPHIS, TN 38119

ADDRESS

CLIENT APPROVAL

ANDLORD APPROVAL

IGNATURE DATE

SKETCH DATE 01/07/2018   DRAWN BY: SP

SCALE 1/2" = 1'

FILE NAME EMMANUEL METHODIST KIRBY 01-07-18

P1

New Addition

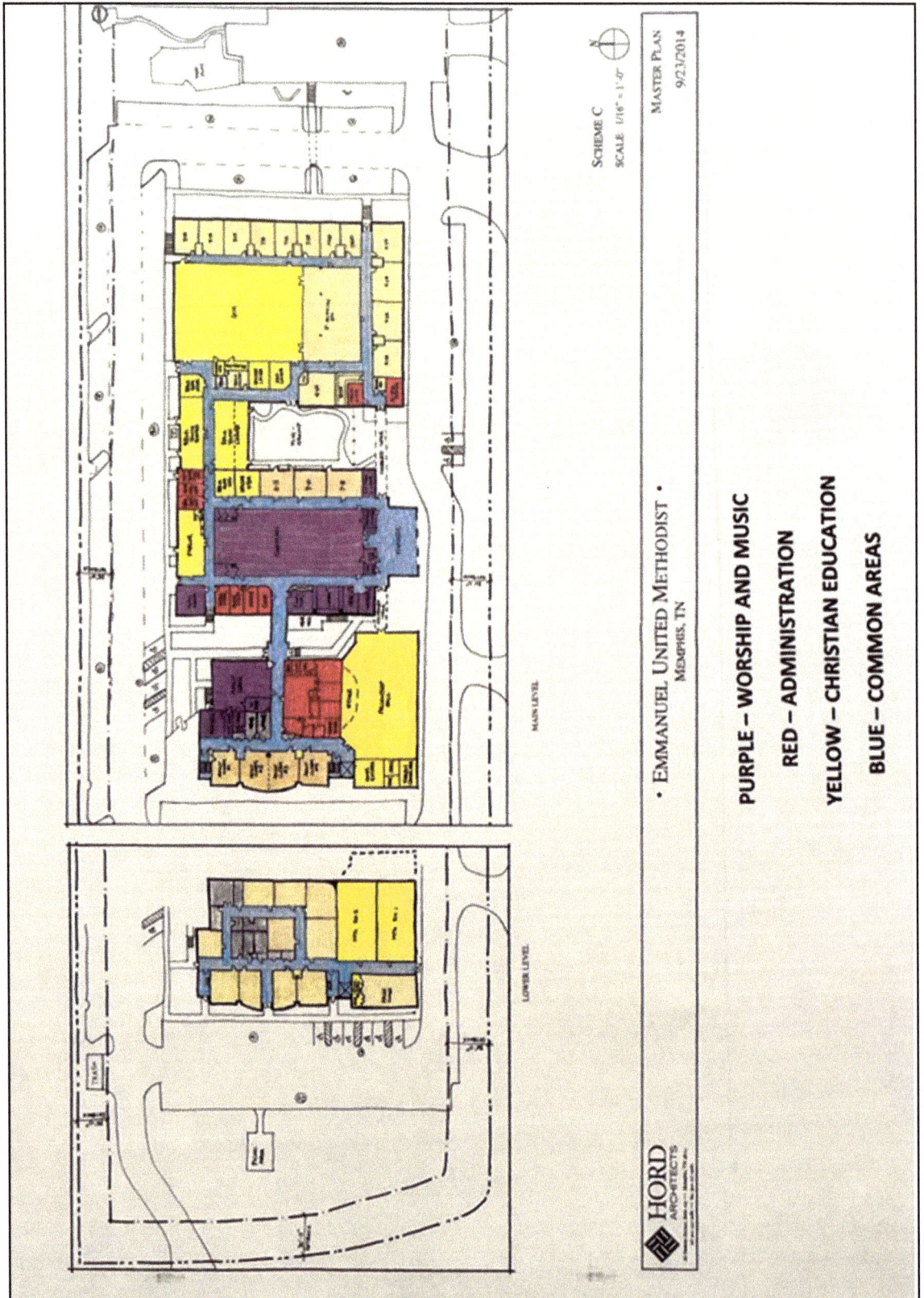

SCHEME C
SCALE 1/16" = 1'-0"

MASTER PLAN
9/23/2014

• EMMANUEL UNITED METHODIST •
MEMPHIS, TN

PURPLE – WORSHIP AND MUSIC

RED – ADMINISTRATION

YELLOW – CHRISTIAN EDUCATION

BLUE – COMMON AREAS

MAIN LEVEL

LOWER LEVEL

HORD
ARCHITECTS

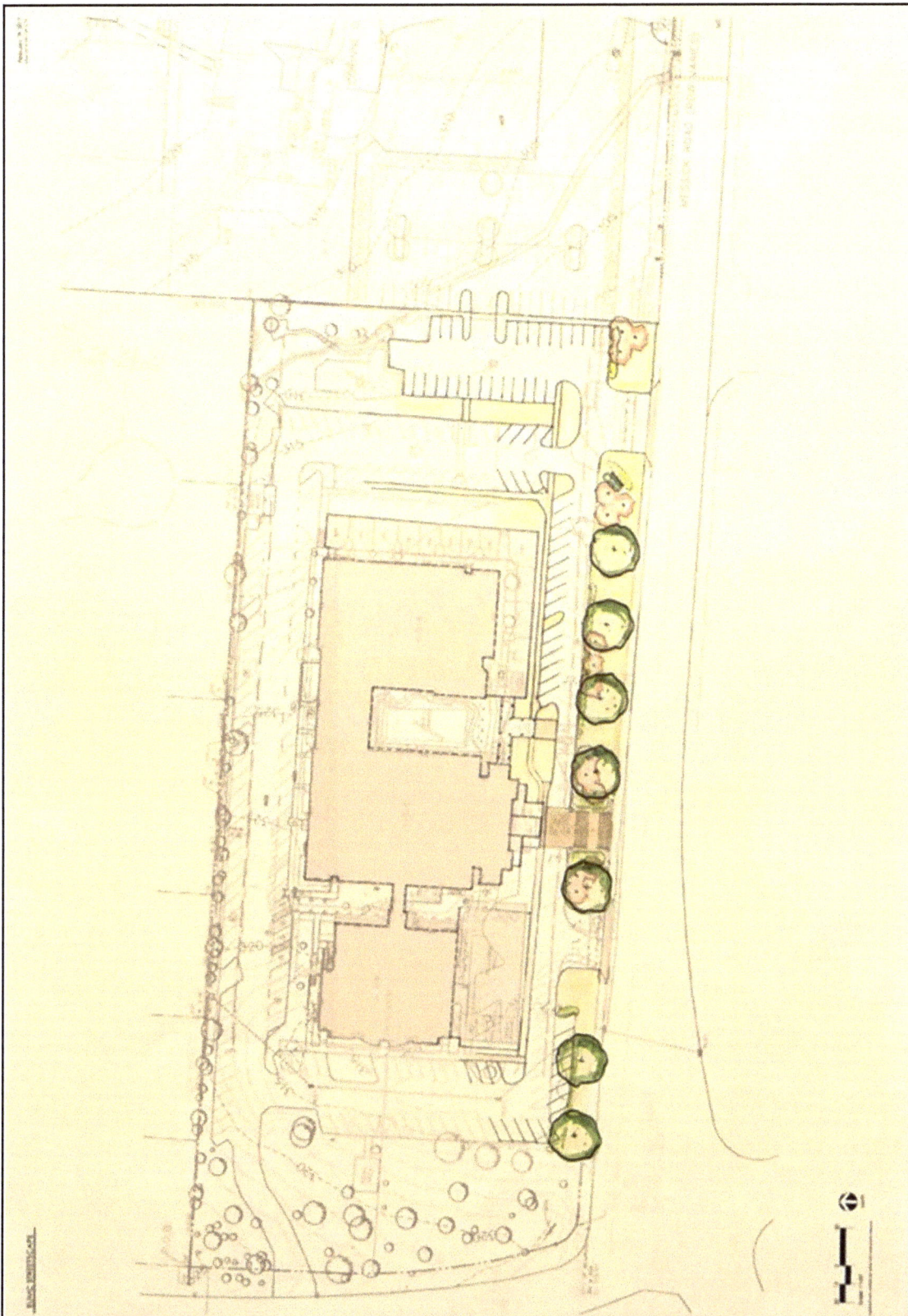

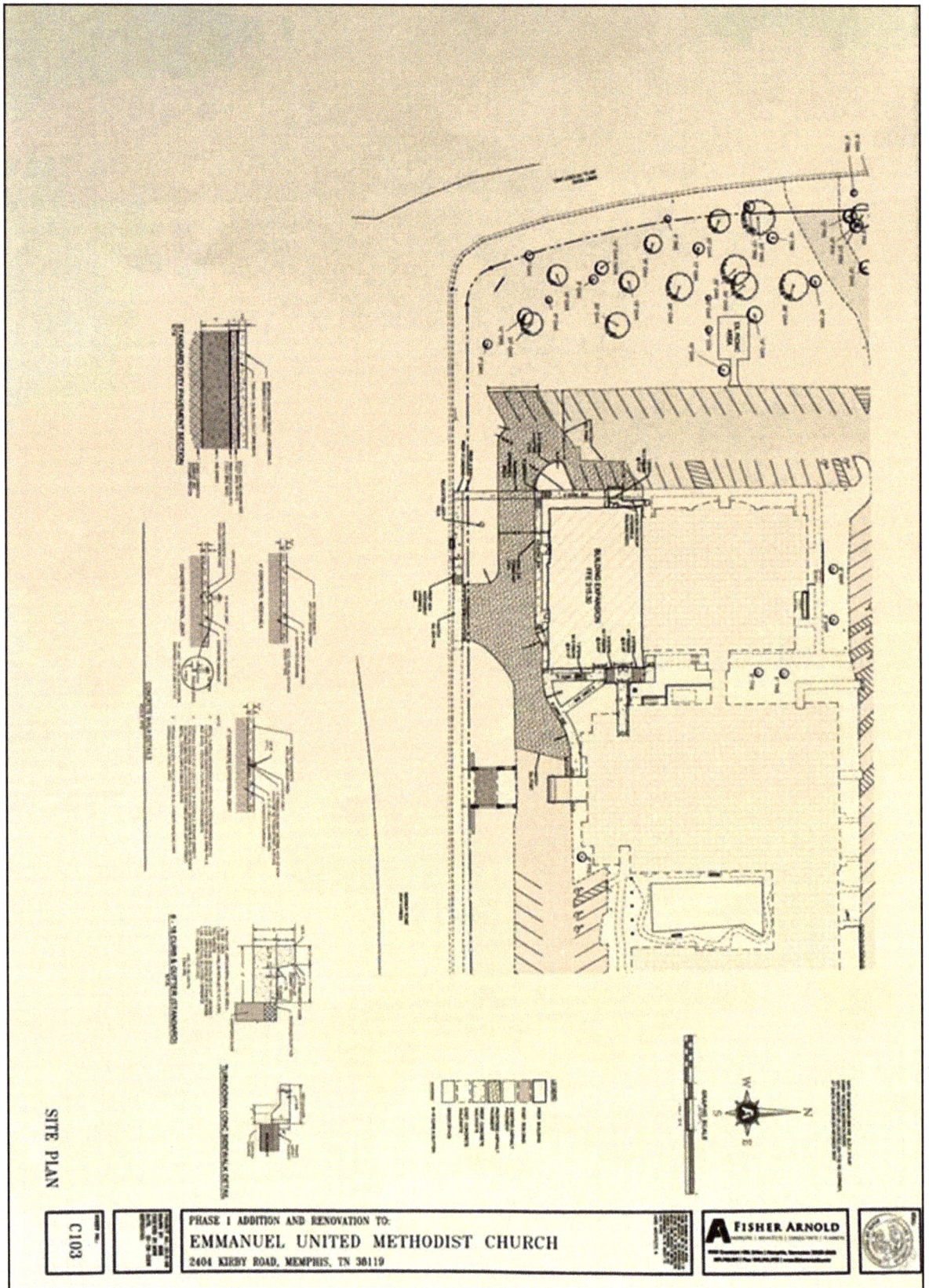

SITE PLAN

C103

PHASE 1 ADDITION AND RENOVATION TO:
EMMANUEL UNITED METHODIST CHURCH
2404 KIRBY ROAD, MEMPHIS, TN 38119

FISHER ARNOLD

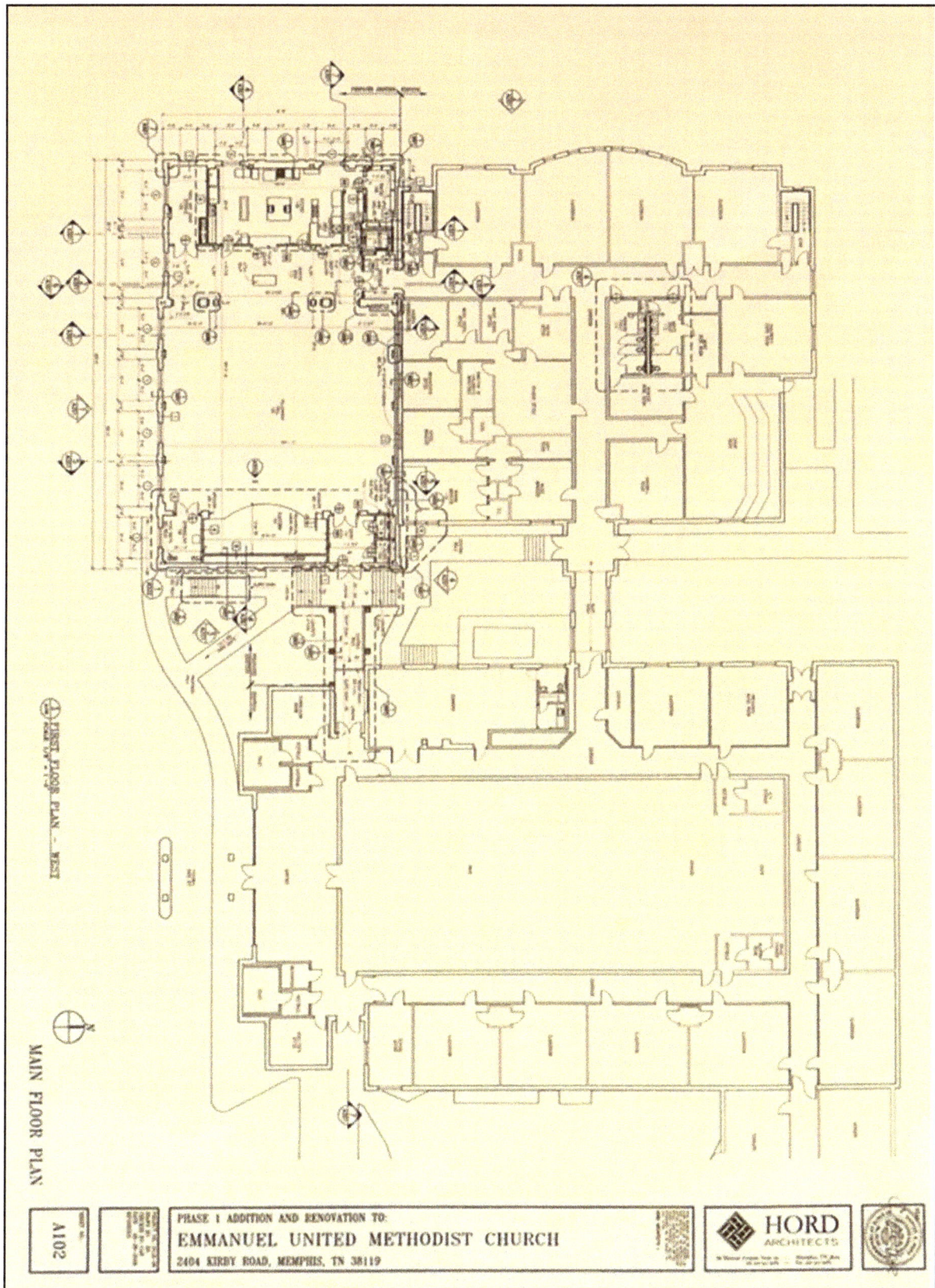

MAIN FLOOR PLAN

FIRST FLOOR PLAN — WEST

PHASE 1 ADDITION AND RENOVATION TO:
EMMANUEL UNITED METHODIST CHURCH
2404 KIRBY ROAD, MEMPHIS, TN 38119

HORD
ARCHITECTS

A102

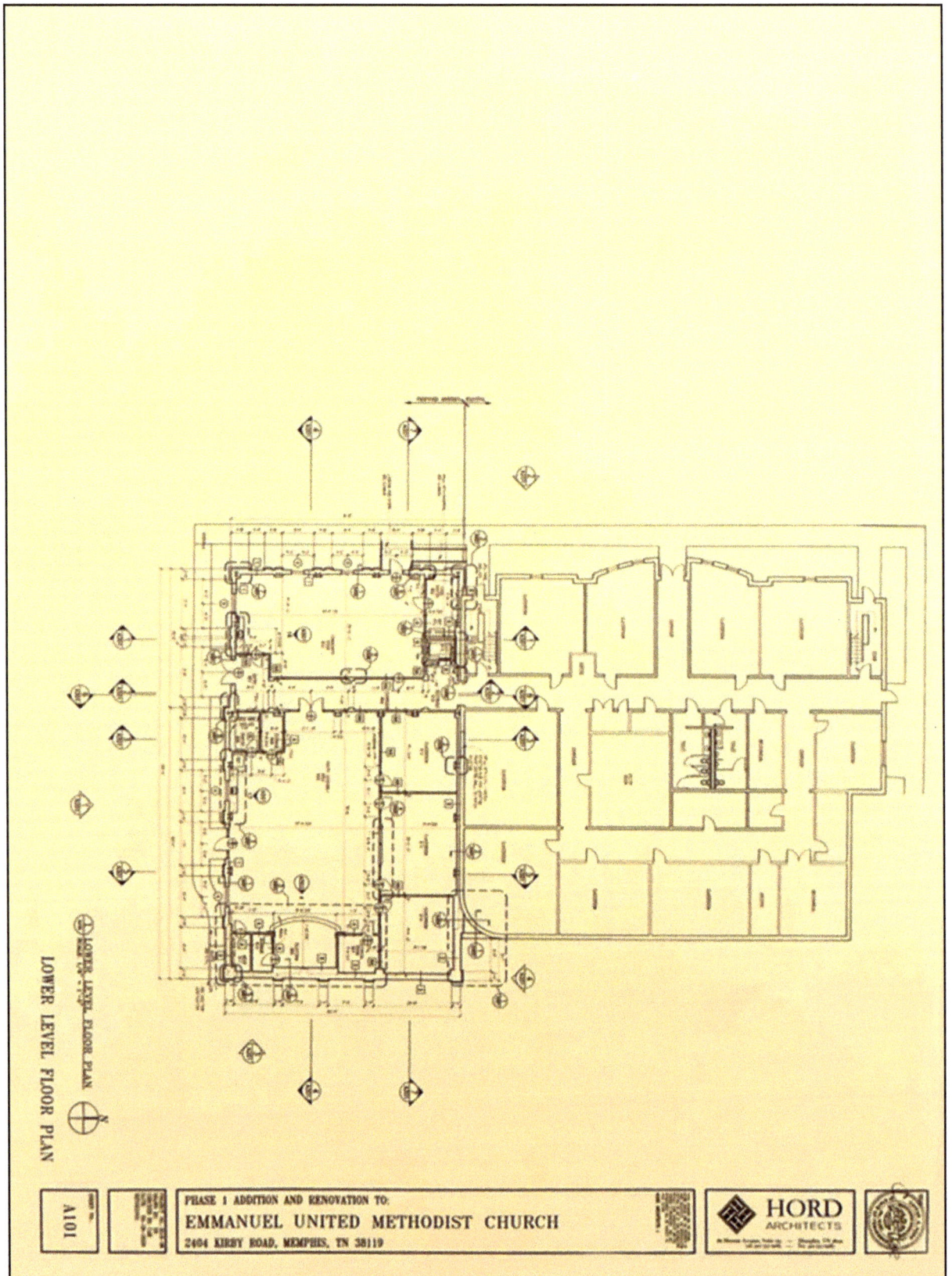

LOWER LEVEL FLOOR PLAN

PHASE 1 ADDITION AND RENOVATION TO:
EMMANUEL UNITED METHODIST CHURCH
2404 KIRBY ROAD, MEMPHIS, TN 38119

A101

HORD
ARCHITECTS

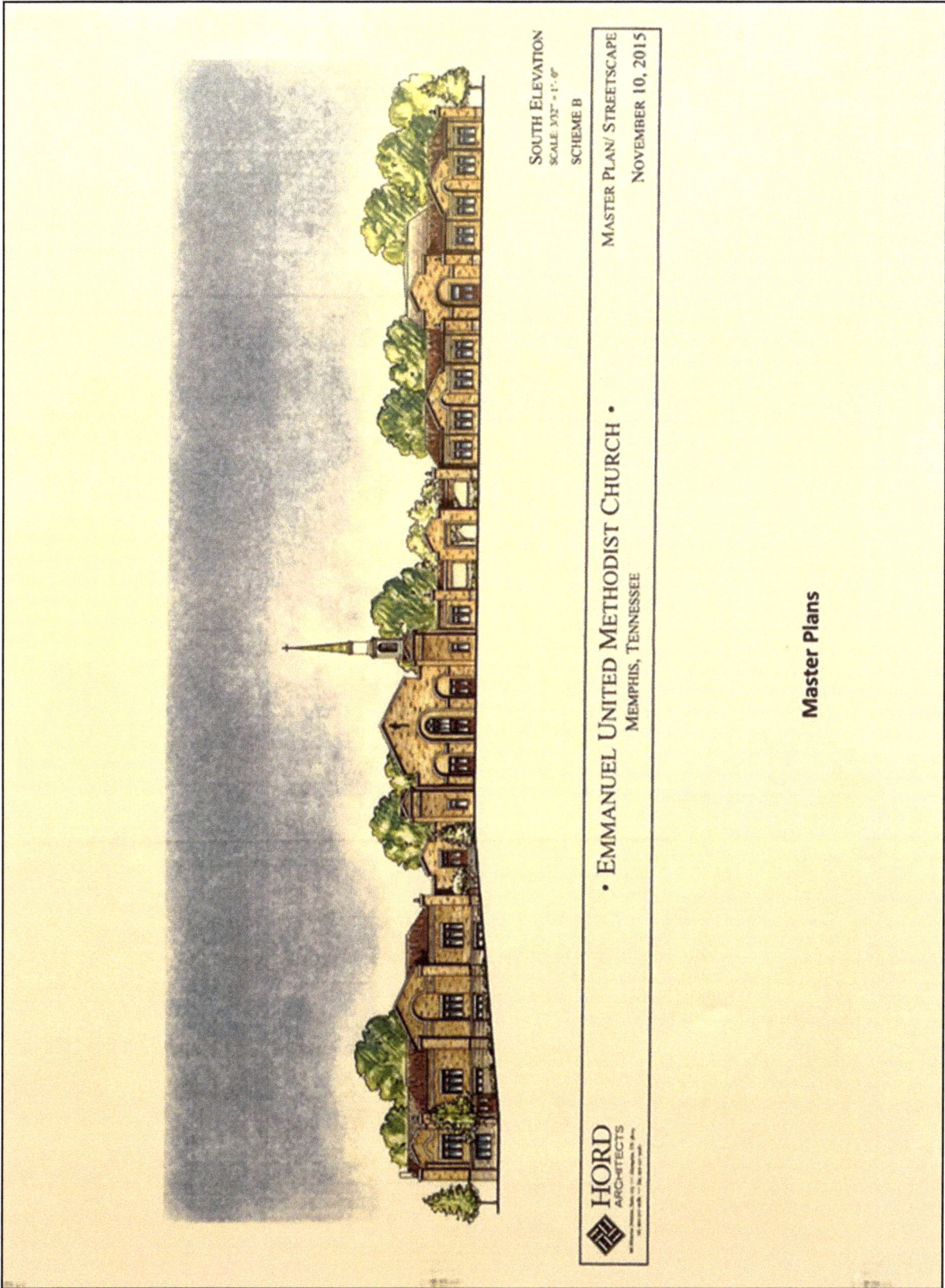

SOUTH ELEVATION
SCALE 3/32" = 1'- 0"
SCHEME B

MASTER PLAN/ STREETSCAPE
NOVEMBER 10, 2015

• EMMANUEL UNITED METHODIST CHURCH •
MEMPHIS, TENNESSEE

HORD
ARCHITECTS

Master Plans

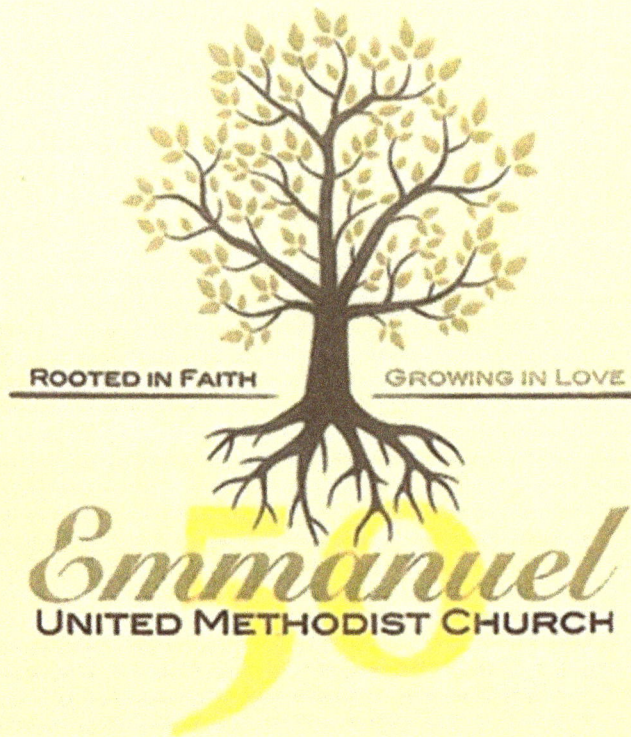

ROOTED IN FAITH   GROWING IN LOVE

Emmanuel
UNITED METHODIST CHURCH

Emmanuel United Methodist Church
is celebrating our 50th anniversary of being
ROOTED IN FAITH AND GROWING IN LOVE

We hope you will join us.
Please save these dates:

SATURDAY, JUNE 2, 2018

4:30 PM – Gathering and children's activities
5 - 7 PM – Dinner under the trees
7 PM – Anniversary Celebration in the sanctuary

SUNDAY, JUNE 3, 2018

50th Anniversary Worship Celebration - 8:30 & 11:00 AM
with a reception between services in the gymnasium

Childcare available during all sanctuary events

R.S.V.P. at emmanuelmemphis.org/50 beginning April 2

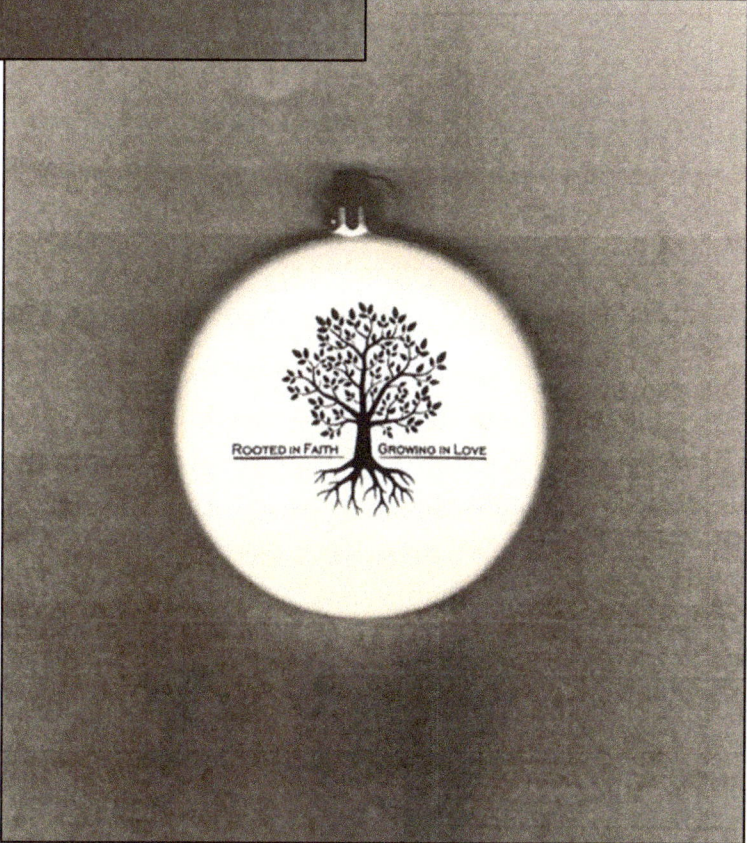

The Present and Future of Emmanuel United Methodist Church

Dr. Cox came at a time when the church was in the early stages of a major building program. With the Building Committee intact and the energies and work ethic of Dr. Cox, the construction moved forward on budget.

The COVID pandemic of 2020 affected everyone in all areas of the country and world. Church services were altered with minimum in-church worship and beginning of on-line worship. Due to regulations and personal preference, a significant number of members chose to worship on-line. While this was a challenge for church programing, participation and income continued to reflect positively. New growth is expected from the new facility.

Emmanuel United Methodist Church's vision to be a Growing and Vital Community Where Christ is Transforming Lives has been the driving force that guided its efforts. Growth creates energy and new life. Vitality signifies purpose and importance. Community is all about relationships and connection. Transforming is about changing lives to be more like Christ. The world experienced significant change in 2020 with Covid 19, but the vision of Emmanuel continues. Emmanuel is positioning itself to be "Growing Forward" by making this a reality.

Numbers and graphs have been included for reference as to the progress of Emmanuel through the years.

The global Methodist Church and other denominations are facing some significant decisions as regards the future. The General Conference of the Methodist Church has yet to decide on the discipline that will be followed. While some Methodist churches have chosen to disassociate from the United Methodist, Emmanuel has not made a decision pending the position the General Conference takes.

The future of Emmanuel will be written in accordance with the love, commitment and service provided by those who follow.

Associate Minister

Reverend Linda Gabriel joined Emmanuel on July 1, 2009. Her appointment was a busy one as she addressed multiple programs and studies at Emmanuel. Through her ministry and leadership, among other responsibilities, the following programs have been enhanced:

- Women's ministries
- Counseling
- Missions
- Pastoral care
- Education
- Bible studies
- Sunday morning liturgy
- Partnering with Belle Forest School

Minister of Music and Worship

Music, as in all Methodist Churches, has played a larger role in the worship, history, and development of Emmanuel. In the beginning, Ben Waller, Jr. assisted with playing the piano and directing the choir. Soon thereafter, Barbara Schutte was employed to assist as choir director. She and Janet Templeton would serve on a part time basis until Anne Burnette, daughter of the founding minister, was employed as the first full-time choir director.

In 1975, Cecile Bell was employed to play the piano and organ. Cecile had no real ambition to accept this position; however, after moving into it, she remained more than 40 years until retirement.

While in seminary at SMU, Anne Burnette had met Kevin Presley who was looking for a position closer to home. Anne pointed him in the direction of Emmanuel. Kevin joined Emmanuel in 1994 as choir director, and the responsibilities of minister of music and worship were added when Kevin was commissioned as Deacon in 2000. In 2003, Rev. Presley was ordained.

During Rev. Presley's tenure the youth choir took many successful tours across the United States. The chancel choir took several domestic and international trips as well.

With assistance from Jackie Spear and others, choir performances are provided throughout the year. Rev. Presley has been influential in getting space allocated to all the choirs for practice.

On special occasions, Rev. Presley will bring in additional musicians for a complete ensemble to perform. Usually, these performances fill the sanctuary.

A choral group of older members known as "The Noiseful Joys" under the direction of Deb Walker, Music Associate, performs in church on occasion and reaches out to nursing homes and other venues.

Visitation Minister

Reverend Lowell Council joined Emmanuel as a retired Methodist minister. He was employed on a part-time basis primarily for visitation. He served during the early nineties under the pastorate of Dr. Hilliard. His presence, along with Ms. Ida, his wife, was a blessing to the entire membership. The parlor that was later converted to a meeting room was completed and furnished in honor of the Councils. Perhaps his major contribution and accomplishment came through his visitation and the program he created and led during his ministry at Emmanuel.

Early in his appointment, he established the "Fisherman Club". This club consisted of approximately twenty men who volunteered to visit new church members, first time attendees, and potential members.

The men worked in pairs and would go to the homes of the potential members, explain the programs offered by the church and invite them to be a part of the warm fellowship to be found at Emmanuel.

It was a requirement of Rev. Council that the team provide a written report of their visit at the next meeting. The church benefited enormously from the contribution of the Fisherman Club. The men who participated also developed lasting friendships from the new members they cultivated and the social climate of the club.

Unfortunately, the club dismantled in 1995 with the retirement of Rev. Council and change in ministers.

Emmanuel United Methodist Church
Senior Ministers – Associate Ministers – Deacons Diaconal Minister

Senior Ministers	Tenure
Dr. Wade Cox	July 1, 2017 to present
Dr. David Comperry	July 1, 2010 to June 30, 2017
Rev. Larry Daniel	September 1, 2007 to July 1, 2010
Rev. Barry Henson	July 1, 2001 to September 1, 2007
Rev. Tommy Edwards	July 1, 1995 to June 30, 2001
Dr. Dave Hilliard	July 1, 1986 to June 30, 1995
Rev. Harold Watkins	July 1, 1981 to June 30, 1986
Rev. Ken Burnette	June 1, 1968 to June 30, 1981

Associate Ministers	Tenure
Rev. Linda Gabriel	July 1, 2009 to present
Rev. Justin Ramer	July 1, 2007 to June 30, 2009
Rev. Scott Alford	July 1, 2004 to June 30, 2007
Rev. Justin Allen	July 1, 2001 to June 30, 2004
Rev. Ray Chandler	July 1, 1995 to June 30, 2001
Rev. Greg Wilkerson	July 1, 1987 to 1995
Rev. Harris Vanderford	July 1, 1986 to June 30, 1987
Rev. Susan Alsop (Atkinson)	July 1, 1985 to June 30, 1986
Rev. David Morrison	July 1, 1983 to June 30, 1985

Minister of Music and Worship

Rev. Kevin Presley   September 1994 to present
Deacon in 2000
Ordained in 2003

Diaconal Minister of Music
Anne Burnette   1990 to 1994

United Methodist Women
of
Emmanuel United Methodist Church

2404 Kirby Road
Memphis, TN 38119
(901) 754-6548

The United Methodist Women (UMW)

Purpose of UMW – "The organized unit of United Methodist Women shall be a community of women whose purpose is to know God and to experience freedom as whole persons through Jesus Christ, to develop a creative, supportive fellowship, and to expand concepts of mission through participation in the global ministries of the church."

- 1869 - The Woman's Foreign Missionary Society (WFMS)
- 1875 - The Woman's Missionary Association (WMA)
- 1880 - The Woman's Home Missionary Society (WHMS)
- 1920 - The Woman's Missionary Council (WMC)
- 1921 - The Wesleyan Service Guild (WSG)
- 1942 - The Woman's Society of Christian Service (WSCS)
- 1947 - The Woman's Society of World Service (WSWS)
- 1968 – The Methodist Women (UMW)

These and other societies form what we know today in the Methodist Church as the United Methodist Women (UMW). The current name came when the Evangelical United Brethren and the Methodist Church united in 1968.

For more than a century, women in the Methodist and Evangelical United Brethren have led a struggle for human rights and social justice. The generation of women who founded the early missionary societies developed powerful networks and organizational structures to help women attain full participation in the life of the church and society.

United Methodist Women is a membership organization open to all women in the church. The UMW members seek to know God and to make life better for women, children, youth, and marginalized neighbors in the ever-expanding global village of today's world.

United Methodist Women participate in meetings, prayer, financial giving, study, action, and service. It is a community of women who nurture and encourage one another in their spiritual growth, personal leadership, transformation, and commitment to expand concepts of mission. At Emmanuel, the UMW actively supports service projects in the community, as well as ministries in rural and global areas.

Because of the faithfulness and courage of the millions of women who supported the work of the early missionary societies, the lives of countless individuals, especially women and children, have been irrevocably changed. Women, children, and youth of today, and the ones who follow, are living the legacy of the women's missionary movement of the 19th century.

Many problems faced by the women at the turn of the century have re-emerged in our own time with a new and demanding urgency, new waves of immigration, racial divisions, threats to the environment, substance abuse and addiction, lack of affordable health care, concerns for the well-being of children and the elderly, public education, questions about women's roles in society, and world peace.

In the early 1970's through the 1990's, Emmanuel's UMW had 4 active circles – New Beginnings (a night circle), Suzanna Circle, Ida Circle (named after Ida Council), and Virginia Circle (named after Virginia Burnette). As more women became employed and the aging of the congregation increased, the UMW was reduced to one active Ida/Virginia Circle that meets monthly for business planning, program information, and fellowship.

The UMW has a long history of supporting the United Methodist Neighborhood Center. Beginning in the early 1970's, the UMW engaged in ministry to young and old at the UMNC site on Looney Street. Some of the activities were:

1. Christmas parties and gifts for the children of the Neighborhood

2. Assisting with Vacation Bible School

3. Serving and assisting with preparing meals for families with food needs

4. More recently, the UMW has provided congregational support, by assisting with Thanksgiving and Christmas baskets for those in need through UMNC. In the last 3 years, grocery gift cards have been provided at Thanksgiving to those in need at UMNC in lieu of baskets. Easter baskets have been provided for the children enrolled at the Miriam Center.

Financial support is also provided to the following Charities.

> Hannah's Hope
> Wesley College/Tanzanian Wesley Education
> Foundation in Tanzania
> Project Transformation
> Golden Cross Senior Ministries
> Lakeshore Camp and Retreat Center
> UMCOR
> Redbird Missionary Conference
> Reelfoot Rural Ministries
> Reynosa Missions in Mexico
> Grace Place UMC
> LaLimye Ministries in Haiti
> Room in the Inn
> Emmanuel Feeds

Presidents of United Methodist Women

Barbara Blount	2011-2021
Phyllis Cecil	2010-2011
Barbara Blount	2009-2010
Gena Moore	2008-2009

Sandra Henson	2007-2008
Ann Vining	2006-2007
Phyllis Cecil	2005-2006
Patsy Hilliard	2004-2005
Gail Wade	2002-2004
Ann Vining	2001-2002
Phyllis Cecil	2000-2001
Harriet Deaton	1997-2000
Debra McAlexander	1995-1997
Jennie Allen	1993-1995
Jane Johnston	1992-1993
Ann Vining	1990-1992
Francis McDaniel	1988-1990
Betty Barton	1986-1988
Barbara Blount	1984-1986
Faye Avirett	1982-1984
JoAnna Haines	1980-1982
Jane Johnston	1978-1980
Mary Freeman	1977-1978
Ann Vining	1976-1977
Donna Moore	1975-1976
Doris Hall	1974-1975
JoAnna Haines	1973-1974
Joanie Tackett	1972-1973
Betty Ellis	1971-1972
Anne Long	1970-1971
Evelyn Vestal	1969-1970
Jane Bodie	1968-1969

Youth

Youth always have an impact upon the growth and performance of a church. This has always been true for Emmanuel. Early in church's history many of the members had youth age children which helped to stabilize that area. Youth directors and counselors also contribute significantly to the development of teenage children within the church. Emmanuel has had a strong youth department through the years and enjoyed more than 100 youth in the department at one time. Several youth, whose parents were not members of Emmanuel, often attended the youth activities.

A change in the youth director often brought changes in the programs and attendance of the youth. The church, realizing the importance of the youth, gave special attention to facilities for them to have their own space.

The youth were eager to participate in work projects and mission projects and would go out of town for service and fun to work on homes for the less fortunate. They also made a trip each year to Reynosa, Mexico to work with the youth in an orphanage. The big event each year was a youth trip to Florida for a week. Here they enjoyed worship activities along with other fun things on the beach. They would get credit for the hours worked on projects within and outside of the church that would reduce the expense of the trip.

Under the direction of Kevin Presley, Emmanuel has enjoyed the youth choral group through the years. Many of these were also participants in the youth group of the church. Through many of the latter years, this group would tour a part of the country performing for other churches.

Part of this trip was funded by the annual "pumpkin patch" sale with the youth paying part of the expense. Money was always available for those who did not have the financial ability to pay their way.

Some youth of the earlier years now have family of their own and continue their worship at Emmanuel.

Emmanuel Youth Directors

Alden Procopio Fowkes	2018 to present
Mario Kee	2017
Karen Riker	2016
Jennifer Niemec	2015
Nathan Wheeler	2013-2014
Steve Stone	2008-2013
Hank Hilliard	1995-2007
Scott Sherwood	1992-1995
Bob Pierce	1989-1991
Dwight Wagner	1988-1989
Susan Springfield	1987-1988
Johnny Jeffords	1986-1987
Susie Alsop Atkinson	1985
Chuck Aaron	1981
David Dunavant	1978-1980
Allen Reiner	1976-1977
Craig Strickland	1973-1975

Cornerstones

Ava Basham, John Bumpers, and Ellen Riker, realizing that the seniors of Emmanuel need some activities beyond the church, formed a group which came to be known as the Cornerstones.

Some of the early members and supporters of the Cornerstones included:

Bob and Ava Basham	Jerry and Nancy Jo Deaton
John and Pat Bumpers	Glen and Dot Fuller
Gene and Sara Callaway	Gary and Mary Hensley
George and Ellen Riker	Bill and Dianne Cook
Dudley and Jane Johnston	Jim and Jane Pugh
Bob and Judith Craig	Don and Merna Keeney
Bill and Martha McLaughlin	Doug and Donna Paine
Bill and Juanna Phillips	Sheila Coleman

This was a very congenial group, and they shared a lot of fun together. The group had a monthly luncheon meeting where devotionals were presented and plans made for future events. The highlight of the group came when two- or three-day trips to Branson, Missouri; Nashville, Tennessee; Little Rock, Arkansas were taken. Later, one day trips to closer venues were made. While the group continues to function, most of the members became too old for travel.

Men's Prayer Breakfast

A group of men led by Don Keeney began gathering on Thursday mornings of each week for a prayer breakfast. An exact date for the beginning is unknown; however, it would have begun around 1990.

After a brief time of fellowship, social activity, and food, the cost of which would come from donations, the formal part of the meeting would commence.

Once the attention of the group was gathered, the meeting would start with the reading of a Scripture and followed by a devotion paralleling the Scripture.

A significant part of the meeting would be the focus of those on the prayer list which would be distributed to all present. After reading of the names on the list, additions or deletions would be made followed by prayer time, led by one of the members.

Prayer cards would be distributed, signed by those in attendance, and then mailed to those on the list on a scheduled basis. Often follow-up calls would be made. Usually, the meetings would be well attended with fifteen to twenty-five men.

This became a great mid-week time for realignment of oneself.

After several years and Don's failing health, John Vaughn stepped in to continue the meetings. The formal meetings have changed through the years and COVID 19 altered the in-person attendance. Notwithstanding this, the group continues to meet regularly and enjoy the social and spiritual program.

Yearly Attendance Averages

Year	Membership	Worship	Sunday School
2020	1408	382	------
2019	1628	356	200
2018	1617	359	201
2017	1706	364	203
2016	1775	371	199
2015	1896	403	213
2014	1917	409	225
2013	1901	396	237
2012	1900	403	244
2011	1905	424	264
2010	1908	421	274
2009	1906	485	324
2008	1902	486	338
2007	2003	483	336
2006	1784	493	352
2005	1765	512	360
2004	1753	532	362
2003	1712	552	391
2002	1686	570	401
2001	1625	551	390
2000	1600	512	353
1999	1575	498	351
1998	1550	530	349
1997	1501	501	354
1996	1495	516	350
1995	1490	510	352
1990	1250	385	320
1985	1200	320	215
1980	975	401	360
1975	553	249	132
1970	260	195	112

Note: The membership was adjusted with the last audit. Each year the membership is analyzed and adjusted upon readings at Church Conference.

Yearly Income Averages

Year	Budget	Received
2020	$1,251,803	$1,246,971
2019	1,264,366	1,265,583
2018	1,248,930	1,235,125
2017	1,250,284	1,261,577
2016	1,257,281	1,195,837
2015	1,250,704	1,044,395
2014	1,274,975	1,257,801
2013	1,330,000	1,301,443
2012	1,306,155	1,329,466
2011	1,529,047	1,229,118
2010	1,377,960	1,260,664
2009	1,449,571	1,200,664
2008	1,456,170	1,425,965
2007	1,439,537	1,448,618
2006	1,403,468	1,317,583
2005	976,126	1,488,749
2004	1,036,495	1,505,023
2003	1,043,000	1,185,253
2002	1,060,579	1,054,441
2001	939,015	999,014
2000	950,000	950,000
1999	919,084	919,0641
1998	$835,700	$835,700

1997	841,426	841,426
1996	766,232	766,232
1995	745,000	745,000
1994	681,796	682,000
1993	649,481	650,000
1992	590,557	623,580
1991	578,416	601,034
1990	588,773	563,491
1989	496,640	546,644
1988	463,482	502,037
1987	393,662	457,459
1986	375,390	377,643
1985	343,199	353,008
1984	343,367	323,804
1983	397,888	385,685
1982	349,992	334,307
1981	295,630	332,792
1980	254,510	285,093

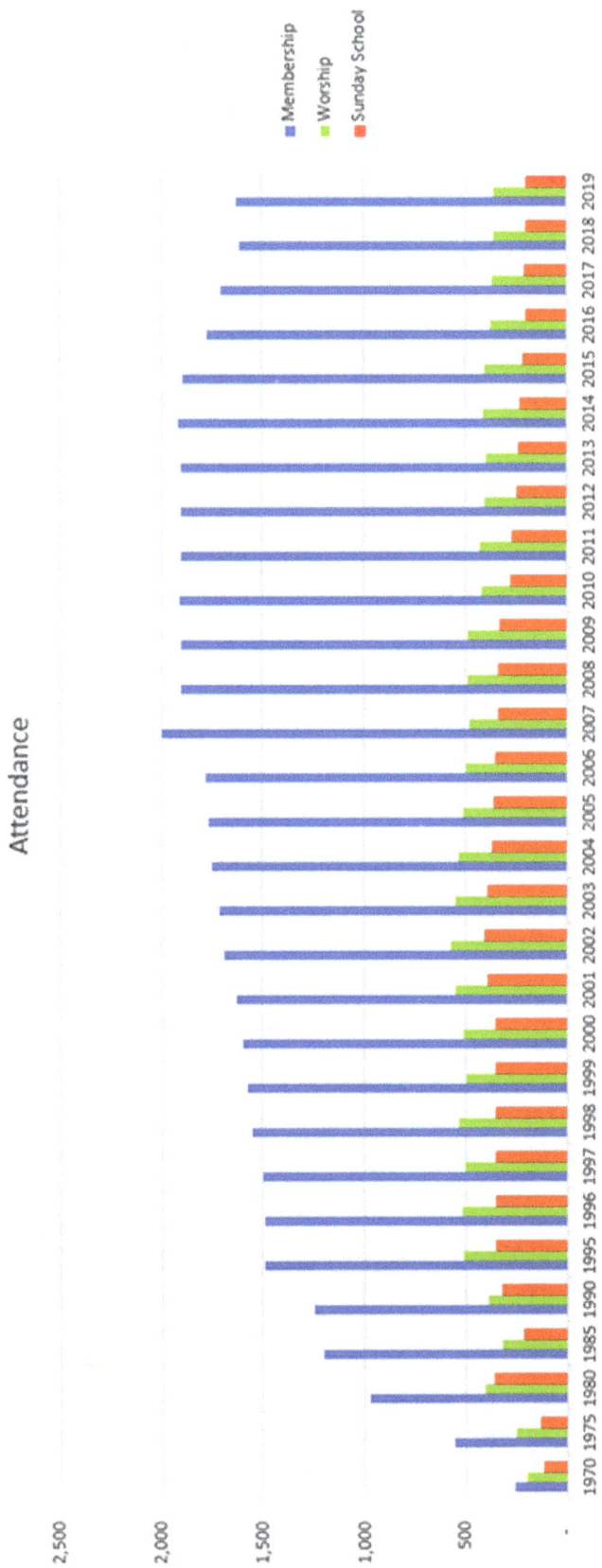

Attendance

Legend: Membership, Worship, Sunday School

Income

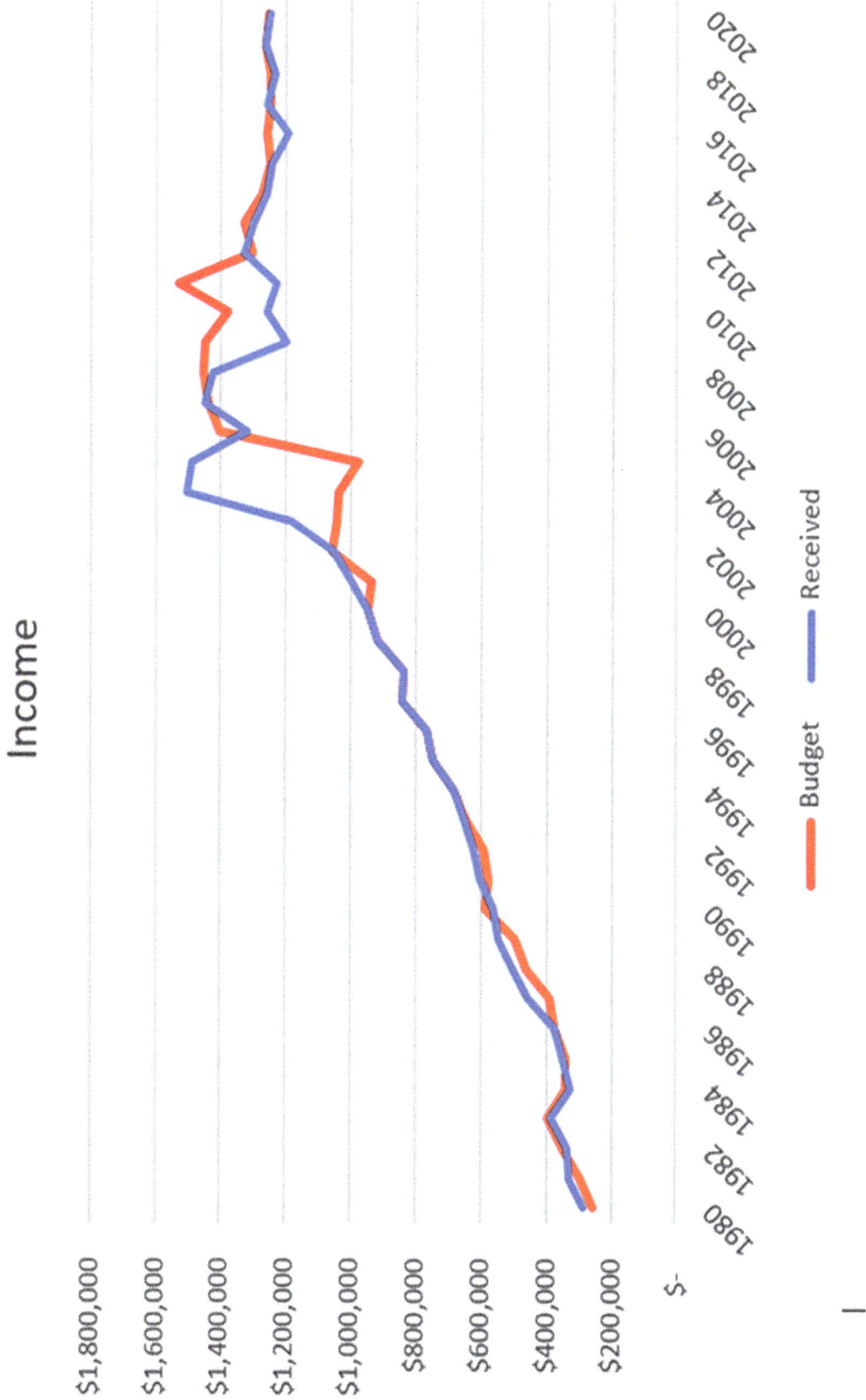

Budget ——— Received

"OUR FRUITS"

The story is told about an unusual tree which grew just outside the gates of a desert city in the Middle East. It was an old tree, a landmark. But more than this, it seemed to have been touched by finger of God. It bore fruit perpetually.

Despite its old age, its limbs were constantly laden with fruit. Although hundreds of passersby refreshed and nourished themselves from the tree, it never failed to give freely to a tired, dusty traveler.

Then one day a greedy merchant purchased The property on which the tree grew. Once He saw the travelers "Robbing" his tree, He built a high fence around it.

Stunned, the travelers pleaded, "Share Your Fruit With Us." Growled the merchant in return, "This Is My Tree, My Fruit, Bought With My Money."

Then early one morning as the first of the travelers passed the old tree, they were shocked to find that, after all the years of helping others; the old tree had suddenly died.

This story reminds me of Emmanuel United Methodist Church. The fruits from the seeds of those early members of Emmanuel have been enjoyed by all who have chosen to come this way and partake of its fruits.

Let us not forget that others too will travel this road and will hunger for the spiritual fruit of our labors.

Precious Memories — How They Linger

Emmanuel before construction of education building, 1989

Sign at corner of Kirby and Messick – Methodist Bi-Centennial, 1781-1984

Emmanuel Quartet – Frank Young, Dr. Dave Hilliard, Ben Waller, Jr. and Shirley Williams, 1989

Groundbreaking for new Education Building – Dr. Dave Hilliard and Rev. Greg Wilkerson, 1989

Emmanuel Kindergarten new playground equipment, 1990

Emmanuel Disciple Class Bible Study "2" Into the Word, Into the World, 1990: Melissa Sloas, Karen Fields, Dick Lender, Dick Barton, Sylvan Meyer, Linda Meyer, Barbara Blount, George Robinson, Bob Archer, Nancy Jo Deaton, Jerry Deaton, Betty Barton

Volunteers In Missions in Jamaica – Nevin Robbinson, Emmanuel Member, and Bill Gaddis, Grace Member, 1990

"Faith in Action" Capital Fund Kickoff Dinner at Woodland Hills Country Club, 1991

Bible Class at MIFA Christmas Store, 1991

New construction Education Building, exterior expansion of narthex, 1991

New construction of Education Building, Expansion of Narthex, 1991

Worship in gymnasium during construction, 1992

Ribbon Cutting for new Education Building, Clyde Moore and Jerry Deaton, 1993

Twenty-fifth Anniversary Celebration, 1993

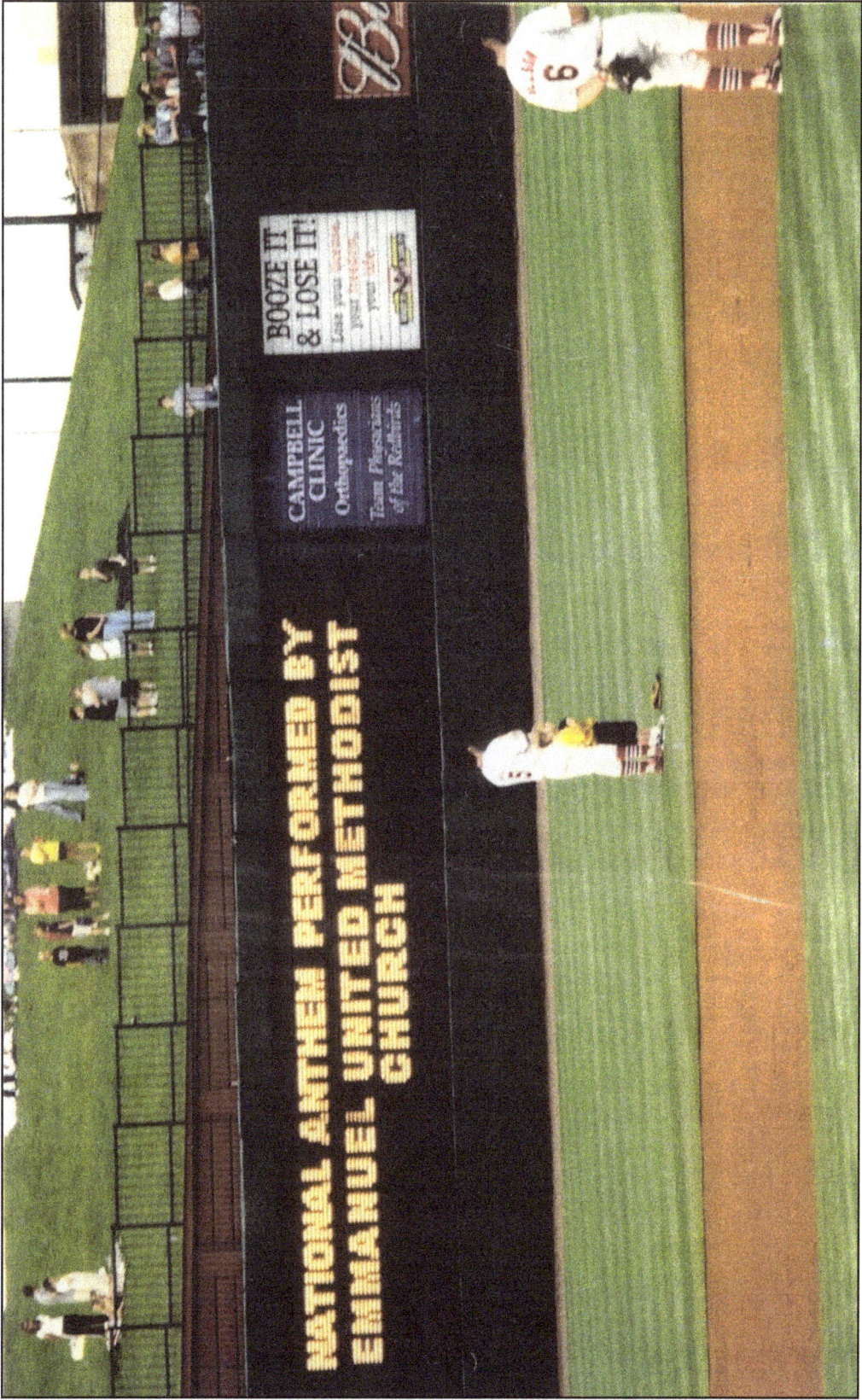

Redbirds baseball game; Emmanuel Cross Notes sing national anthem, 1993

Dedication of newly purchased land, Dr. Dave Hilliard, Minister, 1995

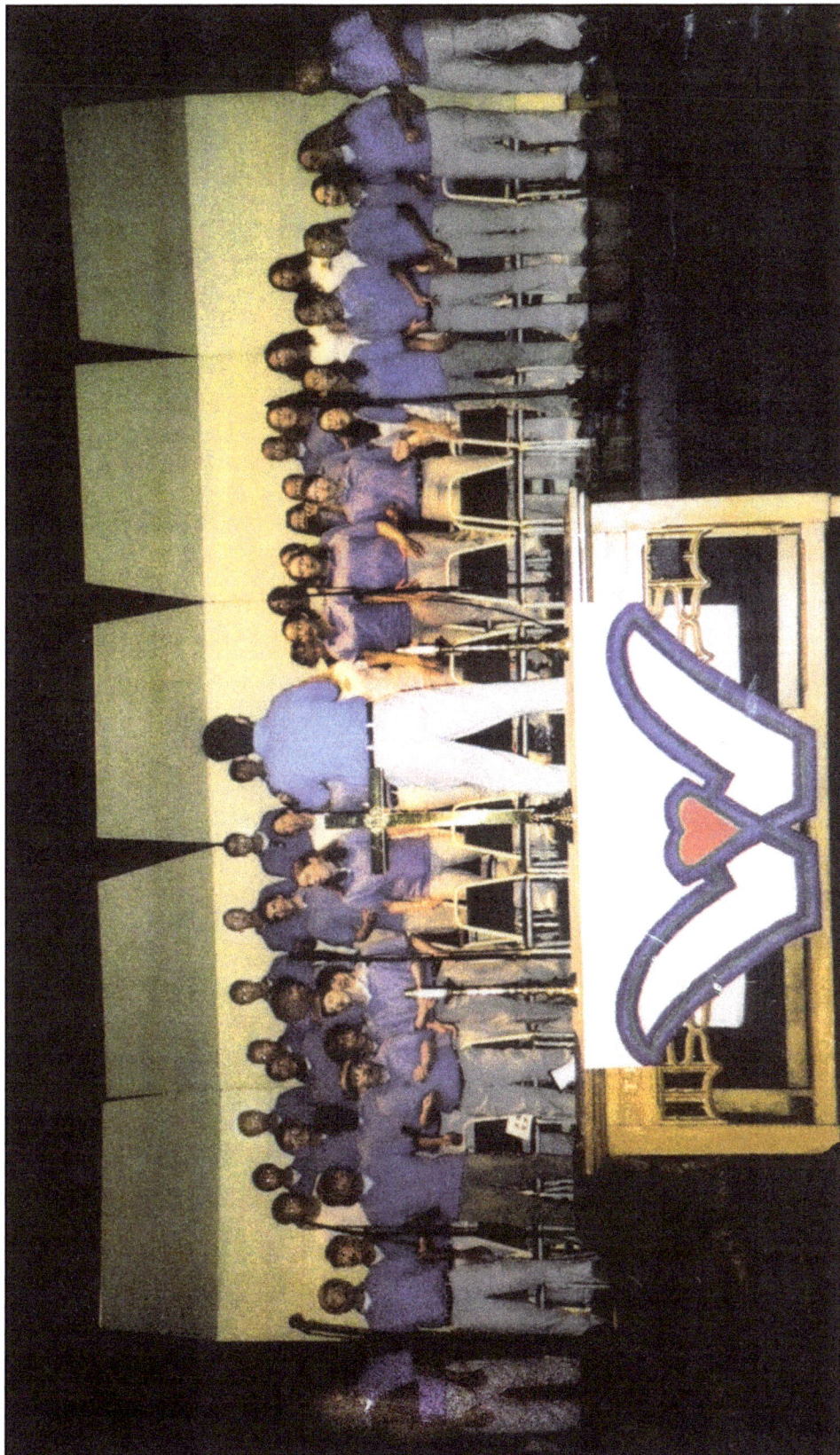

Cross Notes Youth Choir singing at Annual Conference, 2004

Easter Worship Service – Ministers Rev. Barry Henson and Rev. Justin Allen, 2004

Cornerstones Christmas Luncheon, 2004

Men's Breakfast Club, 2004

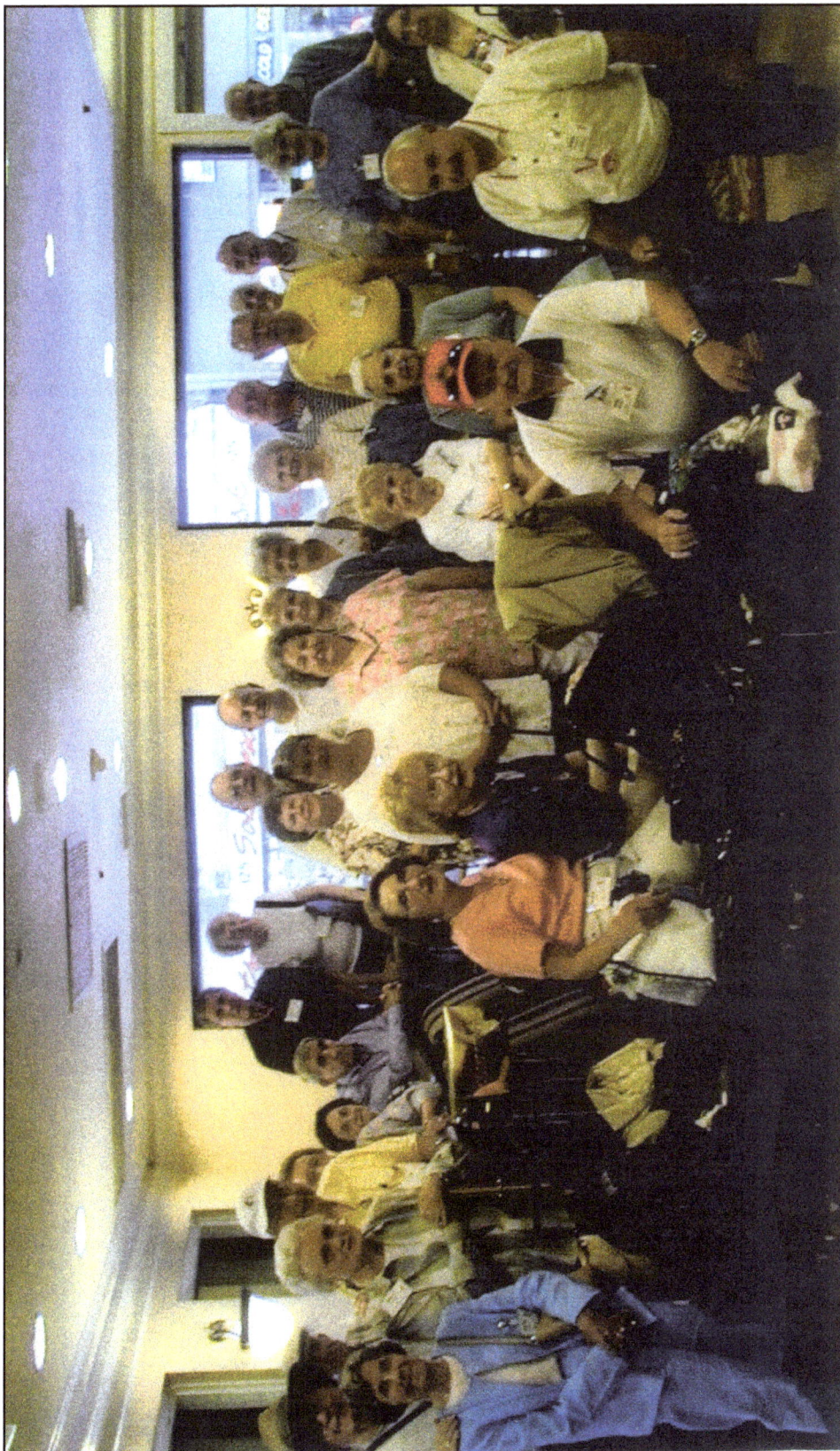

Cornerstones New Orleans train trip, 2005

Bill McLaughlin and Selena Henson with Hurricane Katrina refugees, 2005

Children's Basketball Team, 2005

Children's Basketball Team with Coach Tom Deaton, 2006

Noiseful Joys Choir singing at Wednesday Night Dinner, 2005

Confirmation Class, Dr. Wayne Hamm and Bob Basham, Mentors, 2006

The Lord's Supper Portrayal, 2006

Annual Conference Delegates, 2006

Wednesday night dinner, Ministers Rev. Barry Henson and Rev. Scott Alford, May 2006

Emmanuel Vacation Bible School , "The Market Place," 2006

Emmanuel United Methodist Church in 2022

Warnock Pro and Birch on LSI 70# archival white
Type and design by Karen Paul Stone

www.ingramcontent.com/pod-product-compliance
Lightning Source LLC
Chambersburg PA
CBHW062009150426
42812CB00013BA/2584